toxic/empathy

JL Herald

Preface

I had always been drawn to poetry and the short form of telling a story – much to the exasperation of my Year 6 teacher – apologies Mrs Landon!

I have used poetry throughout my life to explore my feelings, to write things down, to get it out of my head.

This collection covers almost all my life, an exploration of the toxic people I encountered and the toxic traits they displayed; how I came to notice them and the effect on me. Learning to come to terms with my past has been a long hard journey. Each one – my mother, my husband, my friend – had a profound, but devastating, impact on my life. While toxic, they have been also a trigger for my growth.

How to use the references: The toxic trait identified in each poem is identified at the top of the page, and the bottom identifies the person it relates to. Each toxic trait is defined in a toxic behaviour dictionary at the back of the book

toxic/empathy

First Printed 2024

Australia

Cover Design © JL Herald 2024 with image from Adobe Pro

Illustrations from Vecteezy Pro

ISBN: 978-0-6459915-0-5 (paperback)
ISBN: 978-0-6459915-1-2 (eBook)

Website: http://www.JLHerald-poet.com

To my children

Natassja, Terry, Lucas, Kiara and Kayl

and

Kayleigh

I love you, I always will.

To the three people I write here

My mother   My husband   My friend

I wish that you find
whatever was missing
that made you act
the way that you did

Toxic people do toxic things

They don't care if they hurt you

Empathetic people care too much

About people that are around them

When toxic and empathy come together

It can be very destructive

As toxic will use empathetics' traits

To control and manipulate them

Toxic knows that empathy

wants toxic to be happy

So toxic will lie and cheat,

intimidate and threaten

Anything to get their way,

they really just don't care

They will sit there and hold responsible

Empathetic for believing lies

Empathetic must be taught a lesson

To not hold toxic responsible

For all the toxic things that toxic did

as it was all empathetics' fault.

My Mother

· Invalidation · Neglect · Devaluation ·
· Scapegoat · Blame Shifting ·
· Physcial Abuse · Invalidation ·
· Walking on Eggshells ·

My Mother

What does she care about?
What makes her happy?
Clean rooms and faces
and babies in nappies.

What about me
Her youngest daughter.
Does it really matter
That I have fought her?

Of course it does
That's parent abuse!
But we all know
that's just an excuse.

She doesn't listen
to anything I say
She just tells me
to go away.

I want to be a vet
When I finish school.
No, she says,
You'll look like a fool.

How about a doctor
or teacher I say
No, you'll get married
and run away.

Do I have choice?
Of course, I do.
But I know my mother
won't let me go through
with all the plans
I have for me.

First Published:
The Canberra Times
7th February 1993

Frozen

Cold, no longer feeling
Concrete, the step sat upon
Below zero, shorts and t-shirt on
Doors, locked and closed windows
Inside, is not possible
Mother, rules I stay outside
Brothers, told not to help
Frost, forming on blades of grass
Bitter, winter breeze blows through
Frozen, no longer shivering
Detached, mind from reality
Punishment, until dad is here

Black Eye

Eye swollen, black and blue bruising
Trying to see is like seeing through glue
Even opening the lid just a bit
Is painful, sore and feels like it'll split

Brother and I had been out the back cricketing
I missed the ball while I was up batting
It rolled underneath a huge hawthorn bush
Prickly, nasty, impossible to see through

We were just kids, and he got so angry
I walked away, as I stopped help looking
Stuff finding that ball, go get another
Cricket bat smacked right across my forehead

My eye swollen shut and ice in my hand
My mother got home and saw what had happened
Her first words to me "What do YOU do to him?
This only occurred because you were provoking."

Sent to my room with ice on my eye
Told to lay down and Dad deal with it
Headaches and swelling, black and blue bruising
My brother's punishment: absolutely nothing.

Lipstick

Spiralling, descending, out of control
        words in lipstick drawn on the mirror
 Everyone at fault but her, so it seems
        blame written in *coral reef* red
Scorning, dismissing the sentences there
        who cares that they threaten death
Declaring to everyone all around her
        those words in lipstick - definitely not hers
Screaming words said under breath
        yelling words at herself and at others
Swearing, abusing, with lipstick in hand
        smearing red words all over the mirror.

Did Not Matter

I learnt my lesson far, far earlier
then all my other siblings
that it did not matter how hard you worked
mother would never be happy

I remember the day clearly
my Year 5 end of year report
I worked so hard that entire year
trying to make my parents proud

My report card was amazing
the best report I'd ever receive
my report was almost all top marks
all A's down the line, just a B in PE.

My teacher praised my consistent efforts
the work I'd put into assignments
the consistently high mark in all the tests
wishing me well for my future success

I thought you'd be proud, I thought you'd be happy
gave you the envelope, waited on the reaction
I got crushed by how you responded
all my efforts completely disregarded

"Your teacher doesn't know you
this report is just made up
your teacher's confused you with someone else
there's no way that this is right"

All my effort throughout that year
completely dismissed and ignored
I would have gotten a better reaction
if I had received all C's

Tempest

A black cloud descending
as she walks in the house
everyone senses it
scatter like mice
moving away slowly
sanctity in their rooms
mother is home
and she's in one of her moods

Tiptoeing around her
try to avoid talking
the smallest little comment
will set her off raging
sister gestures something
that she finds offensive
that bad mood she was in
turns into a tempest.

Yelling and screaming
abusing my father
calling sister names
denigrating her character
wild eyed and shrieking
threatening bodily things
everyone avoiding her
and then the phone rings.

Mother is pleasant
and mother is nice
never realise a minute ago
she'd been threatening life
a nice conversation
a warm, even tone
the bad mood she'd been in
would have never been known
when the call finally finishes
her mood shifts so fast
the eye of the storm
has definitely moved passed.

Out Of Control

Maths exam tomorrow
Table in my room
Books and pens and paper
Concentrating on equations

Whirlwind of anger
Screamed obscenities
Study books hurled around
Mother is now raging

No more studying,
And no more table
No more pens and
No more paper

Mother is shouting
I've had enough
Closing the door
Maths can get stuffed.

Fees

Excited to accept a university offer
four years of study for a degree that would please
signing up for lectures, bought all of the books
approaching my mother to pay for the fees

A part of my parents' divorce agreement
father would pay for my brothers' school fees
my mother took on responsibility for mine
what happen next - I didn't foresee

Dropped past to see my mother to ask
gave her the bill, and requested her card
she looked astonished, as if I was cracked
gazed at me, opened her mouth and just laughed

I only agreed that I'd pay for your fees
as you weren't smart enough to be accepted to Uni
your father would spend all his money and more
I would pay nothing, your fees are absurd

That you'd get accepted was not going to occur
the funds set aside, that money's all gone
this isn't my fault, I can't pay this bill
go ask your father, he's got money to burn

The bill in my hand, a shocked look on my face
what do you mean the moneys all vanished
you had an agreement, signed off on the line
how could you take it, that money was mine

If you want to blame someone, look at your father
it's clear you prefer him over your own mother
your fees aren't my problem, its yours to resolve
that money was mine, the agreement's dissolved.

A Letter to My Mother

I do not know if you are still alive
I do not know where you stayed
none of your children have spoken to you
for more than over a decade

We got tired of hearing how
you continuously blamed
my father, your ex-spouse
for all the wrongdoings your life

The reason that we all cut you out
was not due to my father wish
but your own words, your own actions
the things you did to us

Sometimes I do wonder
if you ever think of me
of the actions and the words
that you threw in front of me

Of the three toxic people
that I've had within my life
I hold a little sympathy
for the hurts within your past

toxic/empathy

Your own father was a monster
took advantage of your sisters
you were always completely mute
if he had done the same to you.

By taking into account
the likely traumas that you faced
I can feel some empathy
for the anger you'd misplaced

I guess what I'm trying to say here
that if you ever get to read this
feel free to finally reach out
I'm prepared to come and see you.

My Husband

· Belittling · Constant Criticism ·
· Invalidation · Controlling · Physical Abuse ·
· Stalking · Financial Abuse · Devaluation ·
· Parentification · Grandiose Ego · Manipulation ·
· Neglect · Constant Need for Validation ·
· Lack of Empathy · Sabotaging Events ·

To Be Loved

When she first met you
she was desperate:
desperate to be loved
desperate to be validated
desperate to feel seen
you took that young girl
moulded her into someone
she did not want to be.

In the end all you wanted
was someone to look after you
you sent her out to work
demand she do everything
she tried to make you happy
earned an income, had your children
bought everything you wanted
but still that was not enough
you did not think her worthy
of receiving any love.

Lawn Mowing

Last November days of spring
summer heat is rolling in
thirty-one degrees outside
grass - it needed mowing

Eight and a half months pregnant
ready soon to pop
but told I was too lazy
with chores around the house.

To prove that I was worthy
to prove I was not a sloth
instructed to get out my arse there
and neaten up the growth

Sat there on the seat outside
a beer held within his hand
instructing me to keep lines straight
mow the lawn as he demands

As sweat started to drip down my face
told - 'see you're pregnant not disabled
if I let you sleep in bed today
your laziness I'd enable'

The sun beat down upon my back
as back and forth I walked alone
not allowed to stop at all until
the quarter acre block was mown

Unfortunately, I mowed straight over
a dried-out cauliflower stalk
it hit me in the stomach
it shot up with some real force

He thought it very funny
as I bent over in pain crying
told to stop pretending
and get myself back mowing.

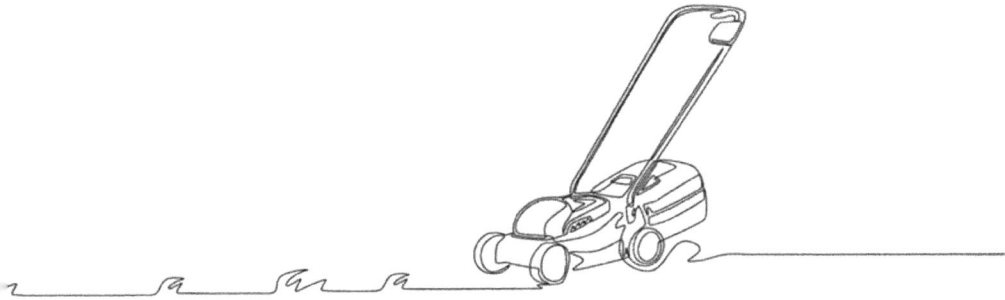

Disappearing

The random words of random strangers
      compliments upon your outfit.
Admiring un-familiars stating
      your visage is quite eye-pleasing.
Clothes that randomly dematerialise
      washing machines that devour dresses.
Dogs that selectively tear fabrics apart
      discerning bleach that eats your garments.
Husband stating over-innocently
      doesn't know why these things happen.

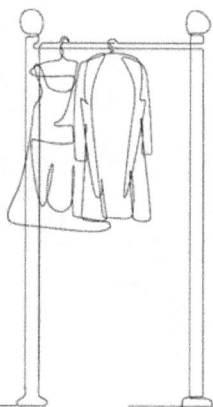

Black Forest

Seven family birthdays
November to January
A barrage of birthday celebrations
A bombardment of birthday cakes

Every single cake served up
Was a black forest cherry torte
Not because the children liked it -
It was the only one allowed

No plain vanilla with strawberry cream
Nor caramel mud cake deluxe
Any other cake that graced the table
Might accidentally be dropped.

Layers on layers of cherry choc torte
With or without the kirsch
T'was his favourite cake of all the choices
That's what we all had to have.

I Dare You

The only time you threatened
to actually, physically hurt me
you did it only one time,
you knew it was a boundary

You were complaining about the way
the kids were treating you
I said something flippantly
that you found so offensive

You turned to me and grabbed me
hand around my neck
pinned me up so that I was standing
on tiptoe against the door.

You knew quite well that I'd always said
that if you ever hit me,
it would be the only time it happened
as I would definitely leave.

Your fist was raised, eyes aflame
looked me in the eyes with rage
and told me I was lucky
you're not going to hit women.

The only thing I felt that time
was complete dissociation
I had come to terms already
that tonight I might be dying

I stared back at those eyes of black
I stared that fucker down
I told our son to grab my phone
call help if I hit the ground

He stared at me, anger vibrating
his rage clear for all to see
and still I stared right back at him
and dared him to just hit me.

I wouldn't show him I was scared
wouldn't show I was terrified
I stared that arsehole in the face
As his rage intensified.

A battle of wills took place that night
in those long minutes that it took
where he was saying that if he hit me
an ambulance would be useless.

I didn't show him any emotion
as I steadily stared him down
I wasn't going to give him satisfaction
to know he was in control.

Eventually I think he knew
that my will was far, far stronger
he backed down, he let me go
that man had failed to break me.

Painted Rooms

Oh, that's different
You painted our bedroom again
Didn't you just do it a couple of weeks ago?
Oh, you didn't like the colour?
Was it to dark or something
I quite liked it; I thought you did too.
No, okay then, nice job.

Oh, again? You didn't like the colour?
You didn't do the second coat before
And thought it was a bit glaring
Fair enough, good job, I guess.

Really, this is the third time in 6 weeks
Why are you painting again?
Changing the décor and the walls didn't match
I don't think you needed to paint
You disagree - well you've almost finished
Good job, it looks nice

Again, really? You've painted our walls again
Do you have some sort of OCD or something
You keep painting the walls every month or so
This is getting weird.
No, I'm not going to praise you for the job you did.

Honey, I'm home! Sorry wasn't feeling well
So came home early to sleep
Why is there a massive hole in our wall?
The kids annoyed you this morning
They weren't getting your clothes out
Or your towel so you got angry at them

But – why is there a hole in our wall
You put your foot through it - why?
The kids were disrespecting you - how?
Its your job to get them to school not
Their job to get you ready to take them
They didn't get your clothes out
So you kicked a hole in our wall
And you think it's okay
as the kids were disrespectful.

You want me to go get more paint
I'm sick, I want to sleep
But there's a hole in my wall and
I'm not happy about what you did

Hold on – how many times have you done this?
How many times have you painted the walls?

Interview

An interview for a new job
     in an area that's interesting
Excited to be in the running
     for a good opportunity

He's angry that his demands
     aren't taken in consideration
The job is located outside
     his stated authorisation

Finding out your location
     by the tracker on your phone
Sending nasty text messages
     demands your boyfriends name

Screaming at the kids
     smashing his device against the floor
Yelling words and swearing
     kicking holes right through the walls

Calling, making threats
     derailing concentration
Contacting the interviewers
     indicating I'm unavailable.

Others

Nothing made it clearer
that I was completely worthless
that you never respected or care about
anything at all about me
then when I sat there with our friends
and you sat there talking about others

Other women that you fancied
Other women you found attractive
Other women that you thought were hot
Other women you wanted to fuck
Other women whose traits and personality
were nothing at all like me

My friends they just stared at you
and looked at me with pity
it was really very sad
that I never ever stopped you

You went out of your way to make me feel useless
unattractive, overweight, and so very, very stupid
continuously telling everyone
that you found me unappealing
telling me to my face and others
that you did not care about my feelings.

One Kilometre

One kilometre is the difference
between a good evening and an awful
one kilometre is all it takes
to turn a 'good man' into evil
one kilometre that is recorded
every day that I get home
every number on the odometer
viewed and written down
the distance to work
and the distance home
should always be the same
no deviation ever allowed
even if milk and groceries bought
every single weekday
and every single week
kilometres added together
cheating allegations made
I go to work, and I come home
never go anywhere else
as every single kilometre I do
has to be pre-approved.

Little Slaves

Expecting the children to make you tea
every time that you demanded
refusing to get out of bed each morning
unless your clothes are out as commanded

Believing that they were responsible
for always being late to school
as they weren't out of bed on time
to get your towel out for you

Keeping one of the children home each day
to keep you company
as you needed them to look after you
and school was useless redundancy

Requiring the kids to massage your back
instead of doing their homework
calling out for them to assist you
to do all your normal housework

The underlying expectation
that children were your slaves
instead of being their parent
you expected them to parent you.

Surveillance

Constant unending surveillance
phone tracker apps enabled
continuously proving location
photos of outside windows

Calls made while in transit
leaving work or leaving home
demanding calls upon each hour
interrupting meetings at work

Contact the moment it's 12pm
speak all through my only lunch break
insisting to know who is around
video used to show all round

Non-stop texting every day
anger if response not instant
demands that I drop everything
if he wanted to be in contact

Never ending surveillance
intrusion in my life
not allowed to do anything
or speak with anyone without him.

Roast Chicken

As the sunrise peeks over the top of the hill
she wakes up to her kids smiling
happy birthday mum! they shout
with hugs and kisses and laughter

Following an exhausting day at work
expecting a nice delight
the smallest acknowledgement from her spouse
would finish up the night

The house is a mess, the kids undressed
dinner not even thought about
no present, no cake, nothing at all
as if maybe it wasn't her birthday

Asking her husband of 15 years
if he a forgotten something
yeah, I know it's your birthday dear
but I have no idea what you wanted

He took the kids and went out shopping
came back with a BBQ roast chicken
happy birthday love, now don't complain
now you don't have to do the cooking.

Yellow Highlighter

Highlighted monthly bank statement
every expense of mine in yellow
demands to know the reasons why
I had spent money being selfish

Three dollars on a single coffee
eight dollars on milk and bread
told I was the reason why
the kids would not get fed

Ignore thousands he spent himself
on amplifiers and audio speakers
name-branded clothing, daily breakfasts
and top of the line ASIACS sneakers

If the children were needing new shoes
ranted about being unable to afford them
kids rewarded with his old holey crap
then bought himself brand new ones

I spent almost 9 months begging
I needed a new brassiere
just one - only thirty dollars
but his budget wouldn't allow it

We couldn't afford it, we were broke
I didn't earn enough to pay for me
his needs came first, the needs of the house
my needs were not important

Access to money regularly prevented
keycards repeatedly went missing
attempts made to re-route my income
denying all of my misgivings

Withdrawing out all our money
spending it on his own thrills
putting some in his own hidden account
me lectured for not paying the bills

Struggling weekly to make ends meet
told to get a job night filling
I could not keep him the way he desired
our financial issues all my fault.

Strawberry Blonde

Fascination with strawberry blondes
    inappropriate comments about children
Over-appreciation of a colour of hair
    views shared about 'alike furnishings'
Discussions aired about the 'best DNA'
    pushing his ideas upon his family
Strawberry blondes are the superior gene
    sons to date within these boundaries.

Speakers

You took more photos
Of the speakers that you built
Then you ever took
Of any of your children

Hundreds of photos of
Inanimate objects
And less than 10 photos
of your children as babies

You preferred other peoples'
Adulations and praise
Of the things that you owned
Or the things that you did

You chased admiration
People compliments
Over doing activities
With any of your kids.

Dancing Monkeys

Come into the monkey house
come and see them dance
all the monkey antics are because
I trained them how to prance

Dance little monkeys
dancing just for me
you would not be where you are
If you weren't my family

See that monkey dancing
see its flexibility
monkey doing everything
as monkey just like me

Monkey dance and monkey draw
show off all your talents
monkey only good at this
as monkey takes after me

C'mon monkey dance again
these people want to see
how smart you are, how clever you are
all because of me

Monkey silly dancing
monkey's very naughty
monkey doing things all wrong
he learnt that all from me.

Pretty dancing monkey
dancing by herself
pretty princess monkey
who got her looks from me

Dancing baby monkey
he's so adorable
I know you want to hug monkey
as you're in love with me.

Dance monkey mother
keep on dancing more for me
your job, your life, your everything
was all because of me

Dance my little monkeys
dance and dance again
perform your little song once more
show how brilliant that I am.

Snarky

Snarky little comments
about cleaning, health, and food
Little nasty put me downs
about my ability to earn

Snarky little assertions
about the kids and washing dishes
Constant little snarkiness
about the way my body looks

Goading snarky comments
I'm trying to ignore
Hurtful snarky statements
remarks that I abhor

Snarkiness on snarkiness
For days and days unending
Until I've finally had enough
Told him outright - fuck off.

The wounded look upon his face
The shock that I had made
Immediately turned and told our kids
See your mothers gone insane

I did absolutely nothing to her
she's angry for no reason
This is why I can't leave you here
You'd be dead within a week.

Birthday Gifts

Pushing to find out what
      his surprise present was going to be
Wanting and pleading to open it
      before his birthday was even here
Giving in and letting him
      open the gift I gave with love
He was overly excited
      he got exactly what he asked
His birthday day was two days later
      woke up and demanded
To know where all his presents were
      told I was being unloving
Pointed out the thousands
      I'd already spent on him
Looked me in the eyes stating
      that wasn't a birthday gift
He didn't get it on that day
      so didn't count at all
If I loved him, I'd go out immediately
      and find a proper gift
He wanted me to be nice to him
      and I was proving I was mean
As I didn't get him a birthday gift
      to open on his birthday
I was a horrible hateful person
      and an extremely insufferable wife.

Jealous D's

Showing off how smart he was
using big words without context
skimming subjects just enough
so he would sound intelligent

Bragging how his high school teachers
knew he was exceptionally clever
so jealous of his intelligence
that they graded him D's and E's

In his warped and twisted mind you see
they knew he deserved all A's
as his extensive knowledge was so impressive
they had to cut him down to size.

Blood

Piercing pain, a hot knife in the stomach
Bent over crying, fresh blood in the toilet
Scared and afraid for the baby you're carrying
Dragging yourself to go find your husband

Request that you need urgent medical attention
Fall on deaf ears as he's busy doing something
Told to wait for at least a few hours
He'll get to you when he's finally available

In pain and in tears, the begging commences
Pleads to assist, the hospital needed
Dismissed, ignored, completely forgotten
He's too busy sanding one of his speakers

You cannot wait, the pain is increasing
He refuses to help, tells you to stop talking
Thoughts in a mess and unable to function
You drive yourself to get medical attention.

Disgusted

Darkness outside
the still silent night
don't know what woke me
it was way past midnight

Straddled over me
pinned down to the bedding
hands on his dick
furiously masturbating

Eyes screwed shut tightly
as he was defecating
wanking and shitting
a mess left on my chest

No comments ever said
no words ever spoken
finished what he was doing
as I lay there frozen

Shattered

A hole ripped through the fabric of my life
a daughter gone; my heart fragmented
the absolute feeling that nothing was right
and nothing would ever be right again.

A young life ended far too soon
my shattered soul existing
a horrible feeling of dark emptiness
an abyss of unending pain.

I held her hand as her life slipped past
whispered words of my love for her
her soul, her heart, her life was gone
my sunshine girl - an empty shell.

Returning from the hospital that night
Numb, hollow, complete devastation
my bed, a haven, possible protection
maybe sleep will help me forget.

But he had other thoughts in mind that night
made demands, insisted on sex
protestations to please leave me alone
but my body was not my own.

It was not an act of love that night
or an act of care or even like
he used me and got off eventually
rolled over, and fell asleep.

Laying in the dark as the hours slipped past
silent tears rolling down my cheeks
wondering whether my life was worth living
that the person who should have died was me.

Bragging

Several old men sitting around having coffee
making rude comments and degrading women
talking in detail about their sexual conquests
the things that they did when she didn't want it.

Bragging about what he did to his wife
how he kept her awake if she dares to nod off
how he wouldn't let her sleep without putting out
whinging and jabbing, he wasn't going without.

Coercing her to have sex when she's sick
vomiting, aching, temp of 40 degrees
demanding she put out even after her surgery
as she cannot say no and he never says please.

He thought himself manly, thought himself tough
he'd have own his way when she was passed out
he would do anything, never asked her permission
just took want he wanted, in any condition.

Break In

The dog's in the laundry, all the children asleep
lying on my bed at 1am reading
comfortably curled up, book in my hand
relaxed, untroubled, and warm in the bedding

A slow creeping feeling of dread rises up
uncomfortable sensation, uneasy awareness
glance up, seeing, who should not have been there
inside of my room, at the end of my bed

Anger in his eyes, just staring at me
saying nothing, glaring menacingly
sitting up, uneasy, wondering if he is deluded
not wanting to anger my ex - the intruder.

All the doors locked; all the windows closed tight
either had his own key or forced a door open
excuse he was checking that his kids were all safe
from the paedophilic boyfriend I apparently had.

Told him to leave, told him to get out
told he was not welcome to be anywhere around
eventually he got it, and he wandered away
my book now forgotten as I was completely unsafe.

Lettuce

Leafy green vegetable
sprouting in garden tall
its growth interrupted
lettuce a weed called

Yanked out unceremoniously
upon compost discarded
poor little lettuce unloved
decaying in the sun

Lettuce got a brief respite
no more rotting on the pears
now belated birthday present
for daughters fourteenth year.

A Letter to My Husband

You chose to abuse your kids
You chose to put them down
No matter what you think
It was not basic discipline

You are not a good father
You are not 'the perfect man'
You will never ever work
Just get handouts where you can

Your children don't respect you
I think you're a prick
In your useless pathetic life
You'll not achieve a thing.

My Friend

· Hot and Cold Behaviours · Pathological Lying ·
· Lack of Accountability · Masking ·
· Manipulation · Projection · Insincerity ·
· Lack of Empathy · Blame Shifting · Coercive Control ·
· Gaslighting ·Twisting Words · Silent Treatment ·
· Playing the Victim · Sabotaging Events · Crazy Making ·

Unconnected

I stood on the mountain tops of Kosciuszko
The wide-open vast alpine plains
I found myself out there in the open
I could breathe and finally feel free.

You'd said I was so similar to you
In the way I was, and how I thought
That I was the first person you connected with
As you had always felt alone

But you didn't identify with the mountains
Or any part of its history
While I became one with the surroundings
You were disconnected from it, and from me.

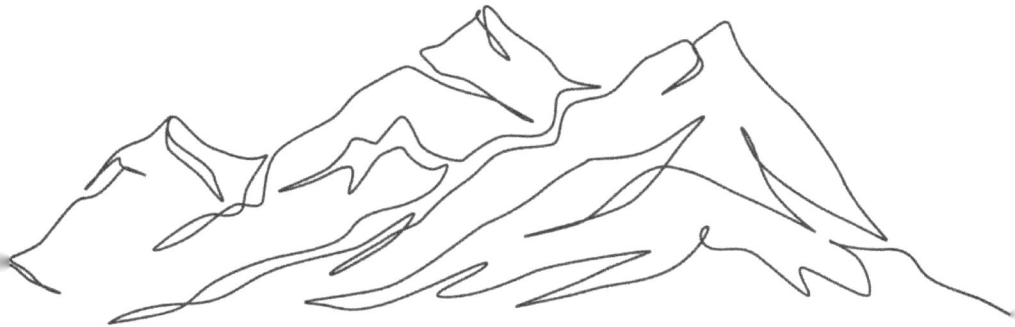

Hot Cold Nice Nasty

Hot and cold and cold and hot
and hot and cold again
Which guy will I get today
which version might you be

Will I get the pleasant guy,
the one that's nice and lovely
Or I will I get the arsehole guy
the one that's not nice but nasty

Will I get the affectionate guy
who says he really cares.
Or will I get the obnoxious guy
who's vulgar and who swears

Will the friendly guy turn up
and sit down with me for dinner
Or will the awful guy show up
and sit there and berate me

When I sent a text message
I hold my breathe unknowing
Whether the response I get from you
will be horrible or glowing

Going out for a weekend together
or even for a ride
Resulted in a week or more
where I'm ghosted every night

Worst was when we'd gone away
spent 12 days in New Zealand
You refused after to interact with me
for weeks and weeks and weeks

Hot and cold, cold and hot
I never could explain
Whether we were friends or we were not
as every day you changed

I could never had stayed with you
as I could not determine
Whether you thought I was nice
or if you thought me vermin

Cold and hot and nice and nasty
heightened my insecurities
Nice and nasty, hot and cold
just made you untrustworthy.

Justified

You justified your need to hurt me
You defended your threats of violence
You did things that you knew were malicious
And showed you felt no remorse
Don't ever try to tell me
You cared even a bit about me.

The Game

Trying to be your friend was
like learning the rules to a game
where you kept changing the rules
without telling me
getting annoyed that I wasn't following them.

I had to learn all the new rules
for the game only you were playing
then once I thought I figured them out
I could relax and know how you would react -
you changed the game entirely so
I didn't know what the game was
or any of the rules.
You went from playing cricket
to playing water polo.

I was always trying to learn
just who the hell you were
your personality kept changing
and I was forever chasing.
You got frustrated with me
told me to stop asking questions
about what you thought
and who you were.
All I wanted was
to get to know you better,

but you had up all these walls
told me to back off
said I had no right to know
anything about you at all

Then in that last argument
you accused me
of never wanting to get to know you
.... what?

Lies

You lied about your income
and you lied about your job
you lied about your history
and you lied about the drugs.

You lied in your resume
and in every interview
you lied to your employers
your colleagues and work crew

You looked me in the eyes and lied
you lied about your love
you lied about everywhere you've been
and everywhere you went

For every lie that fell out your mouth
the truth was never heard
you lied when you made promises
and lied when you gave your word

You lied about almost everything
you lied about your life
and when you were caught out lying
you lied about the lies

Who is this guy, what man is he
when his entire life is lies
the mountain of lies that you have told
I can no longer tell what's true.

And finally, when someone begged of you
please tell me truth, not lies
you looked them in the face and smiled
Then lied. And lied. And lied.

Soulless

Black soulless eyes
within eyes of brown
Empty void of nothingness,
a deep unreachable abyss
Hateful things crawling, shrieking
desperate to escape
Concealed in plain sight
the monster in a mask.

Manipulation

Being generous and charming
while also being dishonest.
Giving your word and making promises
you have no intention to keep.
Being charming, nice and friendly
then flipping and being nasty.
Pointing out all my flaws
but insisting you were perfect.
Making future plans
knowing you'll never actually do them.
Being unreliable on purpose
then blaming the other person.
All of that, and more, my dear,
is complete and total manipulation.

Forgiveness

Kayleigh my love, my daughter
my everlasting pain.
You taught me about forgiveness
about love and happiness.
I need you now to help me find
the strength, to tell me how.

How do I forgive a man that did
something so cruel and heartless.
A man that took my greatest pain
and exposed it to the world.
A man that did not care that
that was not what I had wanted.
A man that decided he did not need
permission to break my soul.
A man that took my grief for you
and told me I was wrong.
A broken man with a broken soul
a man with little empathy.

So, Kayleigh, my love, my life,
My happiness and my sorrow
Tell me how I can be the better person
To find it to forgive.

When this hollow man of nothingness
thinks he did nothing wrong.
This man that thought he had more right than I
to tell the world of you.
No matter if it caused me pain
and grief, and ripped my heart.
A man who left me bleeding
and crushed upon the ground.
Was it too hard for him to say he's sorry
to admit he got it wrong?

Kayleigh, my joy, my life
My happiness and my grief
Tell me how I can be the better person
To find it to forgive

How can I ever look at this man
who told me your death offended?
This man who said I did not deserve
any sympathy for you.
Who told me I was selfish
as on his birthday you passed.
This man that said he was so insulted
and to never again talk of you.
How could he have ever looked me in the eyes
and demand me to apologise?

Kayleigh, my love, my light,
My cheerful sunshine girl
Tell me how I can find the strength
To forgive someone so cruel.

I cannot find it within myself
to forgive a man so blind
to the pain and anguish
that he caused me
by stating he knew best.
Because he was not right
and I was not wrong
my grief is mine to hold
my memories and my love for you
are mine, and mine alone.
No-one gets to dictate to me
who to tell and when to say
and though you have left and I am here
you've never gone away.

So, Kayleigh, my life, my love
My everlasting joy
I cannot find it to forgive this man,
This monster that is he.

Milkshakes

Who would have thought that ordering
Milkshakes would expose
The mask you wear in public
It cracked for all to see.
You knew your girlfriend had trouble with dairy
We'd spoken about it just yesterday
About why she ordered almond milk
As dairy was no good.
For some reason, I don't know why
You ordered a full cream milkshake
When she drank hers and it reacted
You stared, a smirk upon your face
Out your mouth came the words
I'm never going to forget.

You blamed her for your mistake
The order that you fucked up
You made a massive deal that
You didn't know about her dairy issues
That she never ever said and never ever told you
You went on and on about how bad you felt
How it was making you feel crappy
That you would never ever buy again
Evil full cream dairy milk
You never stopped to ask her
If she was needing any help

You never said I'm sorry
You blamed her and blamed the milk

Your girlfriend sat there, gave you sympathy
And soothed your bruised ego
And still you had not stopped your litany
To ask her how she was.
You made an error; you screwed it up
But you would rather blame
The person you had hurt that day
with your own stupidity.

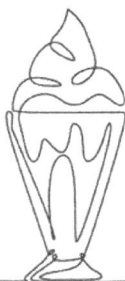

Moron

Someone threatening to hurt you
because they
just want you to be nice to them
is an (oxy)moron

Accountability

Asking about
the promise you made
just last week
isn't throwing
your words at you
or living in the past
it's holding you
accountable
for what you say
clarifying if you meant
what you said -
that's not abusive,
it's not nasty
or to make you feel bad.
Telling me
I'm upset with you for
not keeping your promises
only because
I'd been abused before
is using my past
to avoid your own
accountability.

In Black and In White

You kept on going, through all of the years,
telling me all about your poor memory
how you never remember, couldn't recall,
you'd lose all your things, a personal shortfall.

Funny then how when I asked you about
things that you done that I had found hurtful
suddenly, your memory is 100% perfect
'never did that, never said that, I've made it all up'

Apart from the fact that I'd kept all your texts
I had all your words in white and in black
I had the receipts, so I knew without fail
all the evidence I needed to back myself up

Yet even with that you completely denied
you said all those things, or you acted with spite
if I didn't back down, If I didn't say sorry
you threaten to leave, we'd be finished that night.

You'd keep denying those words that you wrote
the words that I had in black and in white
you'd start accusing me of acting all crazy
confusing you with my abusive ex-husband

I know what you did, I could read all the words
but the constant denying was making me question
I started to doubt that I was reading things right
that maybe my logic and thoughts were mistaken

As soon as I started to question myself
you'd go on the offensive and start to attack
you were tuned in to when I started to stumble
as the doubts started rising, you threw it all back

Suddenly I'm being told it's all me
that I am the one being horrid and nasty
my memory was gone, I was making things up
I apologise now, this is all of my fault.

Twisting

I was accused of twisting his words all the time
Of taking what he said and making it sound worse
It happened so often, so many times we conversed
That I wondered too much if I was losing my mind

So,
What I started doing
Was stopped paraphrasing
I don't think he ever caught on
That that's what I was doing.
I wasn't rephrasing his words
Not a bit, not at all
I was taking his words, copy and pasting
Didn't add anything, didn't take anything
Didn't change a single thing
When I took his own words
And sent it back to him

And guess what he said still -
I was twisting his words
That I was deliberately doing it
to make him sound bad.

So,
If I was not adding anything to his words
And I was not taking anything away either

If I wasn't changing the order,
Chopping them up, adding commas
Just his very words, in exactly the same order.
How I was ever twisting his words?

And,
If he thought that his words made him seem bad
That it made him sound nasty, or hostile or horrid
If I hadn't changed a single thing of his words
What does that mean when he said they were bad?

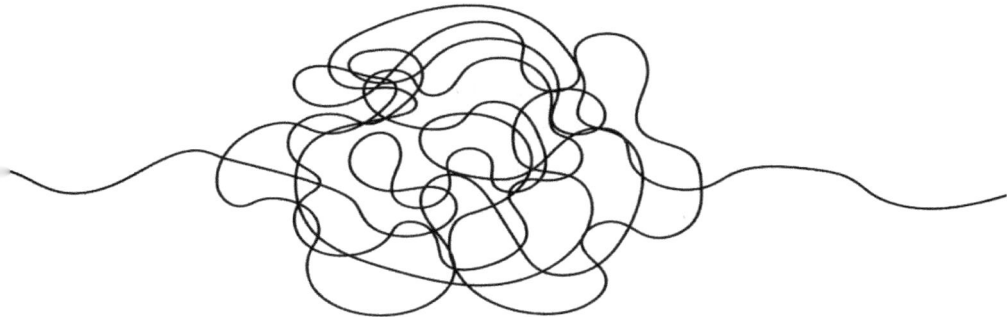

Silence

She sits within a darkened room
devoid of any echoes
this room that he placed her in
because she dared to question

This chamber bare and stark and cold
had no windows and a single door
bereft of any pleasing things
worn out carpets on the floor

Accused of something she never did
raging anger directed wrongly
he had to shut her out from him
she had to learn - to be punished

His silence stretched from days to weeks
apart from reminding her of her error
that she needs to know to be nice to him
or he'll punish her again

So she waits inside this room so bare
his silence overwhelming
and she learns to not bring up things
that are going to make him unhappy.

Victim

How dare they be upset with me
because I lied to them
how dare they think I'm being nasty
as I gave them ultimations

They're being unfair, they're being unjust
they're treating me revolting
all I did was ignore their wishes
and used silence to be controlling

I was going out of my way to help them
by telling them all their flaws
they just don't appreciate my candour
and give me the right applause

Sure, I had to threaten to hurt them
to ensure they'd do things correctly
but now they're being unreasonably angry
I don't think that they respect me

It doesn't matter if I was mean
they should always treat me nicely
as you can see - I'm the victim here
what I did to them means nothing.

Stars

I took you to Dad and Margarets
so you could see the stars
it never crossed my mind at all
that you would be so strange.

You interrupted my dads' explanation
halfway through, as he was speaking
declared tomorrow was a workday
your bed you now were seeking

It wasn't even fully dark
what you said made little sense
you knew we were going to look at stars
what did you think was the intent?

You didn't mouth words of gratitude
you never said goodbye
you just stood up and stalked away
and left me standing, shocked.

What the hell was that, you were so offensive
disrespectful, ill-mannered, rude
Dad and Margaret just looked at each other
as I chased after you

I felt ashamed, I was mortified
but there was one thing that I knew
your actions may have embarrassed me
but they made a fool of you.

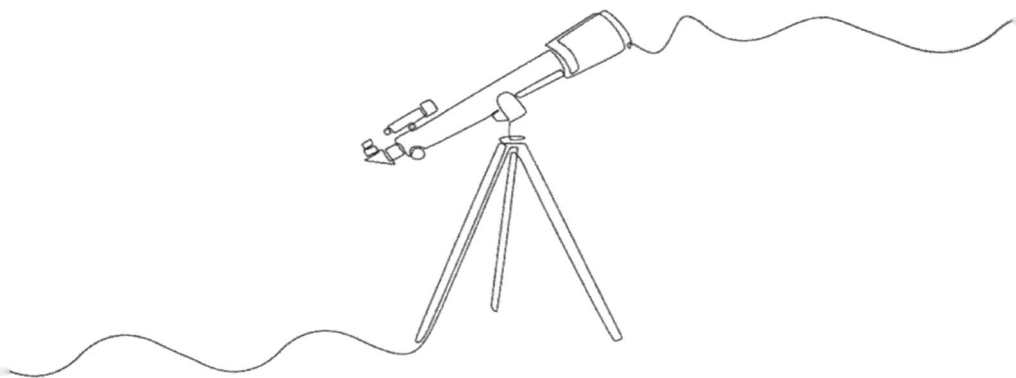

Invisible

The holiday to New Zealand
I had planned just for myself
to celebrate my freedom
and move on from my divorce

You invited yourself to come with me
didn't care where we were going
you went along with what I wanted
rarely made any suggestions

I found out so much later
that you never told your parents
didn't tell them that you'd come with me
that we spent twelve days together

That was my holiday
that you invited yourself on
it was devastating for me to hear
you'd said you'd gone there solo.

That was all my planning
I'd written all the lists.
yet according to the stories you told,
I did not exist.

My Birthday

For my birthday I had decided
To celebrate – I made a choice
All I ever wanted
Was a couple of hours with no noise
An hour or so just sitting in peace
Eating alone just by myself

You found out I was having my birthday
With no-one else around
Said it was sad and disappointing
I'd choose to eat alone

So you invited yourself to join me
You did not give me a choice
Said that you were coming too
And told me then to book

I'd already booked my dinner
I booked it just for one
Over 2 weeks before my birthday
I wasn't doing it for fun

What a mistake I made in caving
Surely, I should have known
I should have held my line
That I wanted to be alone.

You spent the first ten minutes
Ripping me apart
Telling me to go fuck other men
To leave you the hell alone
That I should not have invited you
For dinner with no-one else.

I wanted quiet, I wanted peace
I didn't ask you to be there with me
You inserted yourself into my life
Then ground me in the dirt.

I think you knew you fucked it up
As when tomorrow came
You messaged me and asked me
If your actions made me hate

You knew that saying what you did
Was completely, utterly wrong
It didn't stop you, no, not at all
My present was your rage.

You could have said what you had wanted
Any other day
But you decided to choose my birthday
To smack me in the face.

You fucking ruined my birthday
You selfish fucking twat
I did not invite you to dine with me
As you invited you yourself.

Mum's Birthday

Wanting to cause your mother hurt
by disappearing on her birthday
as you didn't like the way she spoke to you
about something you did yesterday.

She was sick, she was terminal
the last birthday she'd be here
but you wanted to teach her a lesson
about not disrespecting you.

You clearly articulated you wanted
your sick dying mother to be sad
you wanted her to be in pain
on the very last birthday she'd ever have.

Grow Up

Look at me, I've had six children
bought a house, and built a house
work fulltime and do everything
all the responsibility
pay the mortgage, pay the bills
buy groceries, food, and clothes
every person in my house reliant just on me

You've lived at home for 15 years
bragged about having all your washing
and cooking done for you
no responsibilities, no children, no mortgage,
doing drugs, getting drunk
doing whatever the hell you liked
you even thought it amusing that
you were drunk at work: age 48.

Yet you think I was the one
that needed to grow up?

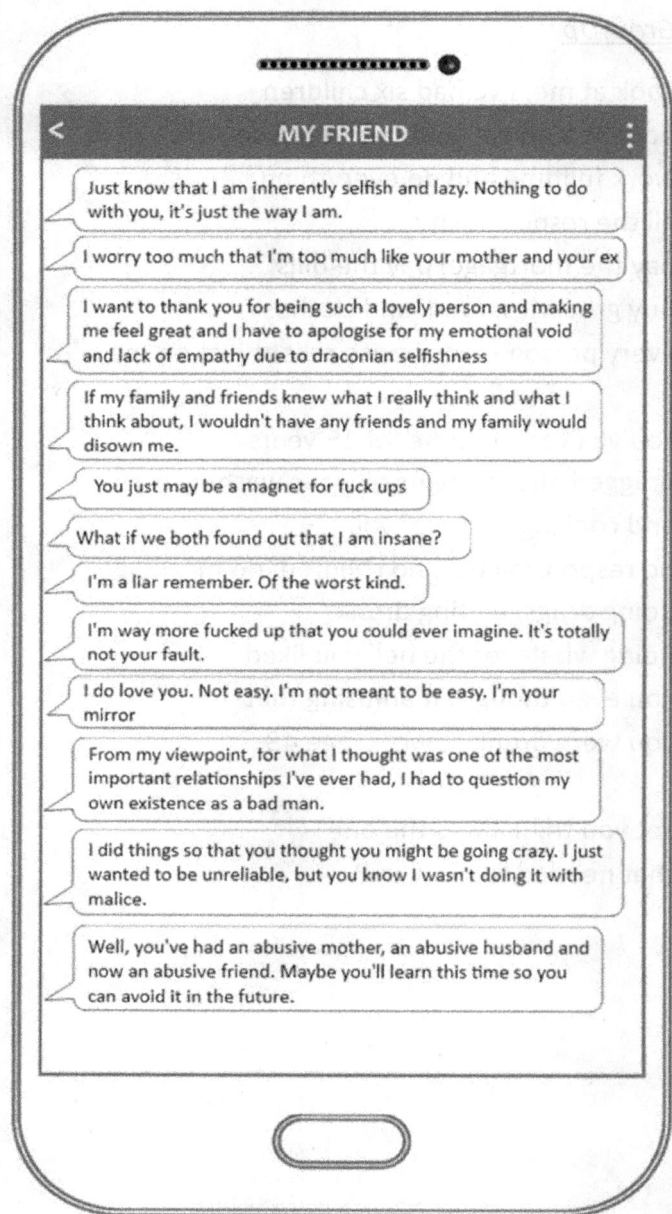

MY FRIEND

Just know that I am inherently selfish and lazy. Nothing to do with you, it's just the way I am.

I worry too much that I'm too much like your mother and your ex

I want to thank you for being such a lovely person and making me feel great and I have to apologise for my emotional void and lack of empathy due to draconian selfishness

If my family and friends knew what I really think and what I think about, I wouldn't have any friends and my family would disown me.

You just may be a magnet for fuck ups

What if we both found out that I am insane?

I'm a liar remember. Of the worst kind.

I'm way more fucked up that you could ever imagine. It's totally not your fault.

I do love you. Not easy. I'm not meant to be easy. I'm your mirror

From my viewpoint, for what I thought was one of the most important relationships I've ever had, I had to question my own existence as a bad man.

I did things so that you thought you might be going crazy. I just wanted to be unreliable, but you know I wasn't doing it with malice.

Well, you've had an abusive mother, an abusive husband and now an abusive friend. Maybe you'll learn this time so you can avoid it in the future.

Delusional Alcoholism

You're having serious paranoid delusions
Due to your overwhelming alcohol abuse issues

Really? I can count every time I've been drunk
Throughout my entire life on less than 10 fingers

You'd have to be drinking as you wouldn't be saying
I'd done these bad things you say I am doing

I don't have any alcohol issues
My kids will tell you that I'm rarely consuming.

I've seen your pantry, all of that whisky
Lots of them open, I know you are drinking

Yes, I've got a significant collection
Doesn't mean that I'm actually abusing

You have to have done; you're acting unhinged
You're accusing me of all these bad things
You're delusional, insane, you're hallucinating
You're crazy to think I've done anything

I've seen you drinking while on the way to work
At 8am before we've gone for a drive
At breakfast, and lunch, and straight after work
I don't think I'm the one with alcohol issues

You know that you're lying, you're making this up
You're throwing your own abuses right in my face
I know that you're drinking far too much whisky
As you wouldn't accuse me of being abusive.

I'm not the one that's been on multi-day benders
Had to have my family stage interventions
I'm not that one that's getting drunk all the time
Your alcohol issues are not bloody mine.

I Did Nothing Wrong

I said that you're a bitch
That you deserved to be alone
That business analysts were useless
I could do your job in an instant
but I did nothing wrong.

Continuously threatened to end our friendship
If you didn't do what I demanded
I told you that you needed to change
That you were crazy and completely insane
but I did nothing wrong

I deliberately started arguments about rubbish
Used silent treatments to shame and to punish
I made sure my words and actions weren't equal
But said it was your fault, as I was deceitful
but I did nothing wrong.

I complained you kept twisting my meaning
Even as I was dishonest and scheming
Used my own definitions to the words I was using
Said you were stupid, as you found it confusing
but I did nothing wrong

I made you promises and gave you my word
Then tried to get out of the things I inferred
You pointed out hurtful words that I'd said
I turned it around and blamed you instead
but I did nothing wrong.

Telling you all the things you needed to change
And pressured you to take MDMA
I badmouthed you behind your back
Told everyone you were crazy and cracked
but I did nothing wrong.

I told you to go to strip clubs and brothels
Learn what men actually want from their women
I threatened you with physical violence
For the smallest things I might find offensive
but I did nothing wrong.

Every time I walked into your house
I criticised you within half an hour
As I'm a 99% perfect man
You're just jealous you're not as good as I am
I did nothing wrong.

Handbag

concentrated anger
disrespectfulness appointed
as compliments given
about my new handbag
as no appreciation returned
and no gratitude offered

history forgotten
compliments received before
not once, nor twice,
15 times over 10 months
exact same compliment
repeated endlessly

handbags not cared about
purchased just for function.
complimented continuously
for something unimportant
expectations of appreciation
for blatant insincerity.

Smirk

Watching disinterestedly
at someone you say you cared about
who's drowning and you're doing nothing
but holding their head under.

Dispassionately sneering
at the person who is disintegrating
as you placed a bomb under them
and helped them pull the trigger.

Nonchalantly ridiculing
someone who called you important
as you loaded bullets in the chamber
and placed it in their mouth.

Contemptuously mocking
people who said they loved you
as you walked away smirking
from the souls that you destroyed.

Being Disrespectful

Being disrespectful is: *Ultimations*
Demanding your new girlfriend comes
on a holiday we'd planned months before
or you wouldn't come because
your girlfriends' trust was naught

Being disrespectful is: *Financial Abuse*
Expecting your friend to cover
half the cost of accommodation
your girlfriend's coming along
three people now on vacation
and calling your friend a greedy bitch
when she wants to talk about re-balancing

Being disrespectful is: *Guilt Manipulation*
Telling your friend she selfish and stingy
trying to make her feel overly guilty
saying to her she's going to miss out
on a $12 cocktail that was to be offered
she's refusing to accept the gratitude extended
for paying $600 towards your girlfriend's expenses

Being disrespectful is: *Selfishness*
Telling your friend to cancel
all the plans that had been made

because your girlfriend's coming now
and she doesn't want plans pre-paid

Being disrespectful is: *Devaluation*
Expecting your friend to prioritise
your girlfriends needs over her own
that she wasn't to make any solo plans
without your approval to be alone.

Being disrespectful is: *Lying*
Agreeing to make decisions
on what activities to book
saying that you gave the activities
to your girlfriend to make a choice
but not actually giving them to her
multiple times telling lies
saying you are also waiting
for your girlfriend to advise.

Being disrespectful is: *Coercive Control*
Giving lists of what not to talk about
making threats to hurt your friend
telling her you'll be watching everything
and judging how she's doing

Being disrespectful is: Constant Need for Validation
Mentioning your friend's promotion

then making it your score
that your friend only managed a pay rise
not from her own efforts, but yours.

Being disrespectful is: *Gaslighting*
Watching your friend emotionally break
and sit there watching, smirking
Saying "I didn't know what I was doing
Was going to have this effect"

Being disrespectful is: *Stonewalling*
Having long conversations
about personal couple things
knowing the third person with you
had to sit there and can't join in
listening for hours and hours
not interrupting you at all
while you go on ignoring them
making them invisible.

Being disrespectful is: *Devaluation*
Complaining about your friend
joining in a conversation
saying she's dominating and selfish
showed no consideration
as she interacted for 2 hours while
she's said nothing at all for the last 10

Being disrespectful is: *Invalidation*
Knowing your friend is crying
saying that you're embarrassed
telling them they're just jealous
of the new relationship that you're in
that her tears were manipulation
she was trying to make you feel bad
that her twisted ankle was hurting
never once crossed your mind.

Being disrespectful is: *Crazy Making*
Being told you've crossed a line
that she's had enough of you
she anxious, scared and terrified
that you might see your threats through
she doesn't want to talk about it
just wants her loan back, and she's done
she's cutting you off and walking away
what has happened has made her run.
Responding with abuse and spite
telling her that she's insane
denying that you made promises
all the words you wrote disdained
playing games with your repayments
throwing excuses why they're late
being disrespectful and
turning friendship into hate.

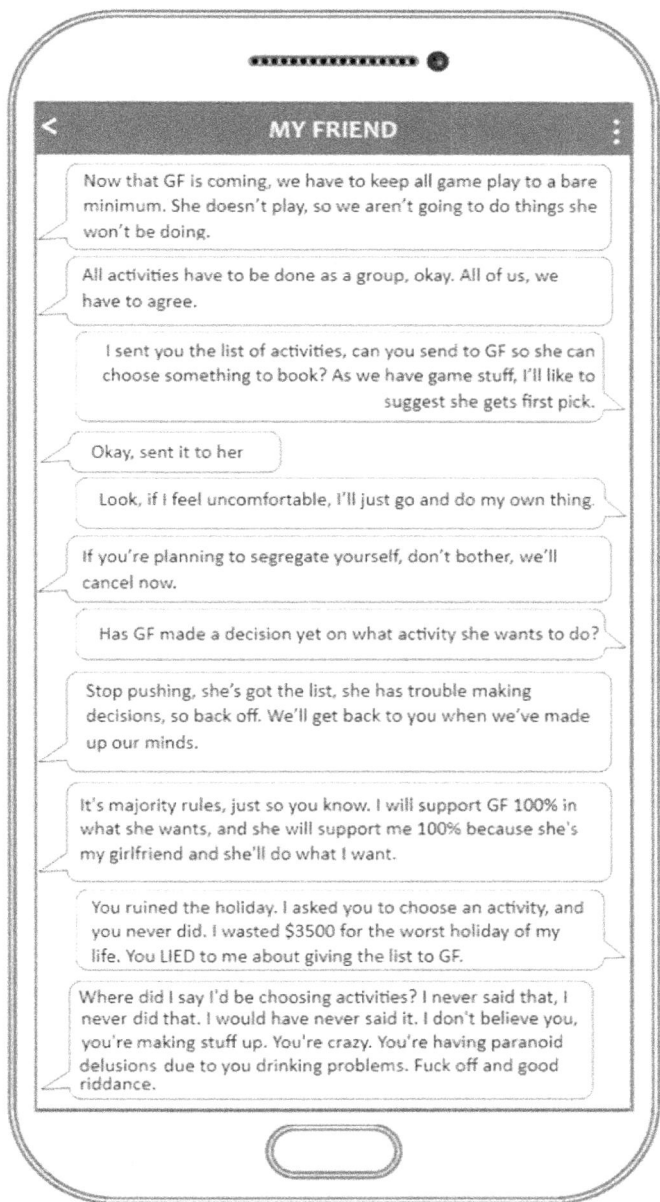

MY FRIEND

Now that GF is coming, we have to keep all game play to a bare minimum. She doesn't play, so we aren't going to do things she won't be doing.

All activities have to be done as a group, okay. All of us, we have to agree.

I sent you the list of activities, can you send to GF so she can choose something to book? As we have game stuff, I'll like to suggest she gets first pick.

Okay, sent it to her

Look, if I feel uncomfortable, I'll just go and do my own thing.

If you're planning to segregate yourself, don't bother, we'll cancel now.

Has GF made a decision yet on what activity she wants to do?

Stop pushing, she's got the list, she has trouble making decisions, so back off. We'll get back to you when we've made up our minds.

It's majority rules, just so you know. I will support GF 100% in what she wants, and she will support me 100% because she's my girlfriend and she'll do what I want.

You ruined the holiday. I asked you to choose an activity, and you never did. I wasted $3500 for the worst holiday of my life. You LIED to me about giving the list to GF.

Where did I say I'd be choosing activities? I never said that, I never did that. I would have never said it. I don't believe you, you're making stuff up. You're crazy. You're having paranoid delusions due to you drinking problems. Fuck off and good riddance.

toxic/empathy

Limerick

There once was an old man from Crace
Whose soul was as scarred as his face
So many lies he did tell
That he was destined for hell
As he screwed up all others headspace

Haiku 1

Whisky coloured eyes
Disguise non-existent soul
Void of empathy

Haiku 2

You were once my friend
Bike rides, whisky, and laughter
Vanished memories

Haiku 3

Friendship is caring
Hatred is threats, lies, malice
Assured destruction

A Letter to My Friend

You were Mr Grumpy
I, Little Miss Sunshine
I was cheerful, friendly, happy
you evasive, grouchy, chatty

You lied to me from the beginning
at the dinner at XO
and continued being untruthful
from pretty much go to whoa.

You knew all about my past
my mother and ex-husband
the damage that they wrought
things I'd become accustomed

I ignored red flags waving madly
focused on good things you did
you could be gentle, kind, and generous,
and appeared to actually listen

But you belittled me, and put me down
said nasty things about me
those red flags turned to threats
intimidation and ultimations

toxic/empathy

You weaponised our friendship
used it to attempt to control
how I acted, what I did
what I was allowed to say

I walked away from you one time
and then ran away in fear
as you'd known I been abused before
and chose to abuse me too

You tried to use threats to make me
fear of losing our friendship
but all you managed to do
Was make me afraid of you.

And FYI – telling someone that
you have them under surveillance
that you have lots and lots of people
watching everything they do

That everything they do online
and every email that they send
that you were watching everything
that's one hundred percent abuse.

My Self

Awakening

· Reactive Abuse · Cognitive Dissonance ·
· Hyper Vigilance · Dissociation · Insomnia ·
· Rumination · Trauma Bond · Internalising Blame ·
· Awakening · People Pleasing · Smear Campaigns ·
· Self Doubt · Losing Trust ·

This chapter explores the realisation that the person you knew was behaving in toxic ways, acknowledging what they did and effect it had. Those experiences created trauma and the signs of that are there if you know what to look for. The behaviours detailed here are clear signs of someone that has suffered from toxic behaviours towards them.

No More

I tried to look right past it
I tried to make it work
but every time I looked at you
I saw your capacity to hurt.

You didn't care you'd caused me pain
didn't care that I had cried
didn't care that you were scaring me
didn't care if I had died.

Didn't care that you'd broken me
didn't care I lived in fear
as long as I did what you told me to
you didn't care about what you did.

Hurt People Hurt People

One of the awful things about abuse
when the victim gets pushed too far
when they're hurting and they're lost
they eventually push back worse.

They start being nasty
commence being mean
as people that are hurting
just want to hurt to leave

They lash out at what's hurting them
sometimes with real spite
so if their abuser knew how they felt
they'd stop their hurt of them

This doesn't ever work,
you fell in their trap fully
as an abuser will take this pain
and show others you're a bully

I know that you are hurting,
depressed, angry, confused
you're feeling flawed and guilty
that you turned and hurt them too.

Dissonance

An almost empty shell ruminates
        on the miasma of ruined relationships
Duality of reality warring inside
        tearing the edge of sanity
Thick fog obscuring truth and lies
        indistinct dim shadows flickering
An all-consuming black void eating
        distant memories of hope.

White Van

walking along the path
next to the road
a white van is coming
driving towards me
fuck – is it him?
heart rate increasing
quick check the decal
oh, crap a VW
what's the numberplate
I can't see
too far to read
do I turn
do I run
maybe he hasn't have seen me yet
what do I do
head down
cringing
maybe
maybe he hasn't...
maybe it's not....
its closer now
get ready
ready to run
that's not his numberplate
oh my god, its not him
it's not him
it's not him
relax
it's not him.

Lost

Reflected image questioning
     Who am I? Do I know?
Once she was sure, once she was happy
     Am I happy, was I happy?
Beliefs about herself replaced by
     Beliefs of others who know better
Once she thought she knew
     No longer knows what's true
One time sure and now not ever
     The unknown girl in the mirror

The Ceiling

Lying in bed for the fifth night in sequence
unable to sleep, you keep watching the ceiling
your body exhausted but your mind is alert
thoughts running deeply, ruminating on hurt

The quiet night broken by the sound of a car
your heart in your mouth while checking outside
threats that he's watching jumping into your head
the devastating feeling of impending dread

Going to sleep and your mind gives you nightmares
he's outside your house, looming dark on your stairs
he's putting you down, he's angry and vicious
even in dreams - his actions suspicious

Resettling in bed, you try to relax
brain keeps reminding he's threatened attacks
conversations you had playing over and over
trying to work past it - to give yourself closure

So you lie between sheets, staring up at the ceiling
shattered and wanting to stop what you're feeling
too tired to be conscious but too scared to nap
just wanting to sleep, but your mind is a trap.

Sprinkles

You served me up a chocolate cake
with a beautiful chocolate ganache
a multi-layered masterpiece with a
dash of coloured sprinkles
it was a beautiful cake
just what I was looking for
you told me all about how hard
you worked to make that cake for me
watched as I ate a piece
encouraged me to have more
I didn't have time to taste the flavours
as you kept pushing more cake at me
urging me to eat more.

Something wasn't quite right with that cake
the more I ate, the worse I felt
until I stopped wanting that cake
it was making me feel ill
still, you tried to push more slices at me
got angry that I no longer wanted
pieces of my special chocolate cake
you had baked just for me
I finally took a good look
at what I was actually eating
realised that it wasn't a cake at all
its might have looked like one

but it was all pretend, fake
the taste of bitterness in my mouth
the only real thing in that cake
was the lightly applied dash
of rainbow-coloured sprinkles.

Worthless

What's sadder,
  those men that threatened to hurt her
  and told her she needed to change
  that her voice and thoughts
  and feelings were wrong
  that she should be more like them
  that she was at fault for the things they did
  and they knew better than her
  that she needed transform herself
  to be someone who wasn't someone like her

or,
  that she was so beaten down mentally
  that she lost sense of who she was
  that she felt that they were perfect
  and she was just worthless
  that those threats to cause her pain and hurt
  and to tear her all apart
  were completely and utterly justified
  as she truly thought she deserved it.

Empty Promises

Pretty little packaged boxes
tied up with silky ribbons
gifts that he had given to me
filled with love and promises.

Too precious for me to open
just placed around my room
as soon as I was tempted
another pretty box would appear.

The first box soon forgotten,
placed upon the floor
the shiny box just received
taking all of my attention.

Pretty little boxes
piled up around my house
given to me over the months and years
that we had been together.

The gifts they started to peter out
my trust for him diminished
I thought to myself why not now
to see what he had given.

I slowly untied the ribbon
gently removed the paper
taking care to not tear
that gift of him to me.

Carefully opened the box
to see what he had shared
and looked again another time
as there was nothing at all in there.

Glanced at all the boxes
covering tables, benches, chairs
grabbed each one and ripped it
devastation in the air.

Pretty paper strewn around,
torn ribbons on the floor
the only thing in all those boxes
were meaningless empty promises.

Pieces

She gave him a piece of herself as a gift
a small piece of her as sign of their friendship
freely given, without expectations
the same sort of gift she had given to others

He accepted this gift and reciprocated
a gift of his own, but this one was tailored
his piece of him that was different to others
carefully created, his gift of a mirror

She treasured his gift, so she kept it safe
he took her gift, and tossed it away
demanded and insisted his gift to be different
what he was given didn't suit his own interest

He liked this new piece just a little bit more
but it wasn't quite perfect, belonged on the floor
he stomped it and kicked it and let it decay
desired a new piece without any delay

Over and over, she kept on cutting off more
he tossed and destroyed them, parts he abhorred
happy to give friendship, happy to please
to keep him on smiling, she'd do anything.

The pieces of her were piled up the floor
rejected, unwanted, discarded and scorned
still he demanded that she supply more
pools of her blood, streaming out of the door

The more he advised, the more that she changed
striving for happiness, friendship to maintain
running out of pieces of herself she could gift
wondering if she'd ever be good enough for him

She picked up his gift sitting on her shelf safely
the mirror was broken, his gift of him missing
that gift of himself was her reflection but twisted
that small piece of him that never existed.

Walk In the Wood

When first they met and he described
the wooded path they'd follow
the streams of sunlight, majestic trees,
woodland creatures and fairy hollows.

Hand in hand they walked together
thru' wooded paths gently winding
peaceful tranquillity, warm sunlight,
a blanket of care and peace and loving.

'Ere now and then she'd glimpse on through
the gaps between bush and tree
gnarled branches, twisted roots,
a scuttling creature dark and evil.

Hark now, what is that?! she cried
nothing there - he whispered softly
focus on my hand in yours
the streams of sunlight in your hair.

Whenever she sighted things so dark
he'd draw attention to the light
until a blindfold o'er her eyes he placed
and whispered she'd be alright.

Wandering down the path so twisted
his hand dropped away from hers
and still he told her of the light
while she was walking blinded.

Stumbling, tripping, on twisted roots
he denied that there were shadows
and still she kept on trusting him
as branches tore her clothes.

The forest quietened; her trust wavered
could no longer feel him there
ripping off her blindfold, crying
why have you abandoned me here.

Her confused mind grasped upon reality
the woods - an overgrown tangle
evil creatures lurking, salivating
her mind screaming as she scrambled.

Panicked, searching, she ran for him
tumbling into a fetid pond of slime
rotting fruit, decomposing creatures
a decaying pool of all his lies.

A nasty, spiteful laugh transmitted
a gust of putrid wind so foul
sneering at her bad luck and misfortune
for believing that he was good.

Lying, bewildered, in the reeking mud
shreds of dress and clothes and shoes
blood dripping from her injuries
not knowing where she was, or who.

The light dimmed and night closed in
stumbling through nightmares he evoked
moonlight unable to light her way
struggling through tangled undergrowth.

Sheer determination drove her onwards
to find her way out to the light
eventually bursting through the final stand
to save herself from midnight.

Smeared

You never expect to hear the smear campaign
Their nasty little words
the lies they tell to other people
To ensure you're never heard.

I got caught up in
my mother's smear campaign
that she had initiated
to destroy my father's name.
I was only sixteen
when this misery commenced
my mother was telling people
that I was my dad's affair
Imagine finding out your mother
was spreading all these lies
that you were sleeping with her spouse,
your father between your thighs
I wonder now, on looking back
whether she was projecting on me
the things that may have happened
in her own abusive childhood

My husband started early
getting in people's ears
telling them I wasn't maternal
and I hated having kids

I was married to that guy
for almost 20 years
he started that smear campaign
in only the fourth year.
Sixteen years he went behind my back
and said some horrid things
I always wondered why other parents
stayed away from me

He said I was disgusting
never put my children first
that I treated him so poorly
only ever prioritised my work
He never worked at all,
he preferred to stay at home
didn't matter that everything he wanted
I went and got for him
But what I got from him wasn't
thanks, gratitude, or pride
only him making sure that
I could never make any friends.

I'd love to say it got better
when I left that frigging pig
instead, he spread rumours
dominatrix as a side gig
That I loved to tie my lovers up

and whip and slap and hurt them
but more importantly for his smear,
I was doing it for the money.

I overheard him out one day
he was rather loud
telling a guy out shopping about
the "services" I provide
He put my life in danger
and the lives of all our kids
he frigging gave this stranger
my address and all my deets.
I confronted that arsehole then
showed him that I was angry
I told him what he was doing
was actually very alarming
He thought it really funny,
his ridiculous make-believe
told me if I felt unsafe,
to sell my house and leave.

I'd like to say this was the end
of toxic smears within my life
but unfortunately for me
I met that wretched friend
I trusted him, I believed in him,
I listened to what he said.

yet he told his friends and other people
that I was so obsessed
That I wanted him, was stalking him
that I wouldn't leave him alone
he had already started that
well over 2 years before the end
I don't think he ever realised,
I don't think he ever knew
how many times I had already thought
about utterly cutting him loose
By the time I'd finally had enough
that man had made me scared
I cut him off, he crossed the lines,
all my trust for him impaired.

You'd think that should have been enough,
all I was - was aggravation
but no, he decided to go after
my professional reputation.
I didn't think he had it in him
to try to take me down
to tell our other colleagues
on the project we'd been on
that I had written documents
that I had never done
documents that I found out later
actually were his ones.

I lost count of the times I had
to defend myself from smears
that I was blocking projects
by not sharing what I did
Management got involved
I had to prove myself right
that the documents he was saying I did
were never actually mine.

You ask why toxic people do this
what's the bloody point
toxic people want to control
all the people in their joint
because they know eventually
you'll wake up to their shit
dig your heels in, question lies
stop believing that they're good.

So when you raise the things they did
with people that they know
they had weeks or months or years already
being fed their tale of woe.
That you were the abuser.
That you were the insane.
That you spent all your time doing
all the nasty things they did.

Your reputations already trash
these people have been conditioned
not to believe your truth is real
to not believe that you're the victim.

Weaponised Empathy

When you put others needs before your own
focus only on the good things they do
refuse to listen to your intuition
and keep playing down their toxic

You think you're doing the best for them
you're a good friend, a good child, a good partner
by putting their happiness before your own
and making sure they feel supported.

What you're doing isn't good at all -
it's a lesson in futility
by putting their needs and wants foremost
you're destroying your own sense of self

What you're doing isn't positive,
what you're doing is total madness
you're letting them cross all your boundaries
not defending your own happiness

Your empathy is a ticking bomb inside
its been made into a weapon
by focusing on the good they do
you're ignoring Armageddon

You've lost yourself, you've lost your meaning
consumed by their toxicity
as all that you are doing by this
is being toxic to yourself.

Hamsters

Hamster wheels running endlessly
Round and round inside
Sometimes loud, sometimes quiet
But always present, always there
Worthless, unloved, anxiety
Running wheels inside your head.

Hamsters that were gifts from others
Kept alive and being fed
By lies and passive aggressiveness
Unreliability, neglect, and threats

Running, running, always running
Whispering negativity and doubt
Undermining confidence,
killing self-esteem, creating hurt
Those convincing words of others
Feeding the hamsters inside your head.

Broken Trust

Dry sand on the beach in summer
    while a storm is rushing in
Scattered autumn leaves swirling aimlessly
    down empty, vacant streets
Multitudes of broken windows
    within the howling winter winds
Shattered pieces of my soul rebuilding
    in the gentle springtime breeze.

My Self

Healing

· Boundaries · Karma · Recognise the Signs ·
· Actions Show Who They Are · Red Flags ·
· Know Yourself · Acceptance ·

This chapter focusses on working on recognising traits and building back your trust and belief in yourself. Find yourself, be truthful about your own shortcomings, know who you are, set your boundaries, and never let anyone cross those boundaries again.

Clock

My favourite tree out of everything
is the fine leaf Japanese maple:
Acer palmation dissectum
I don't have one in my garden,
and I'll never ever plant one.
Likewise with roses and anything that's red

It seems ridiculous not to buy
the things I like myself
I know that it's stupid
but I've avoiding being told
that I'm buying these things
as I know my ex-husband likes them
if I buy them, then he's telling people
I'm buying them because I still love him
and I still want him
they symbolise my love of him.
So I'm avoiding buying things I like
to avoid those conversations
in a way he's still controlling me
and controlling all my actions
as when I'll go to buy something
going through my mind is
if I buy this am I going to be told
that I'm buying this because of him?

Same with my clock of all things
a large open metal faced clock,
I love my clock it goes with my decor
fits the space and reminds me of a clock
my grandparents once had
my friend looked at my clock
told me I only bought it because of him
it was absolute proof in his mind that
I wanted more than friendship
this clock was a symbol of my obsession

It's a clock. A very common clock.
Nothing fancy, nothing unusual
But apparently me buying
a super common clock
and hanging it on my wall
was proving my infatuation

It was a clock. A fucking metal clock
my taste, my likes, my decision
based in what I wanted.
nothing to do with my friend,
didn't even cross my mind.
I don't even remember the clock
his parents apparently had
the one he said I was copying as I was
'still in love with him'

It was a clock. Nothing more.
No symbolism, no obsession,
no infatuation, no love.
A clock I bought for me,
what he liked was never a thing.

I am allowed to like things
without being told I have some
ongoing infatuation with someone else.

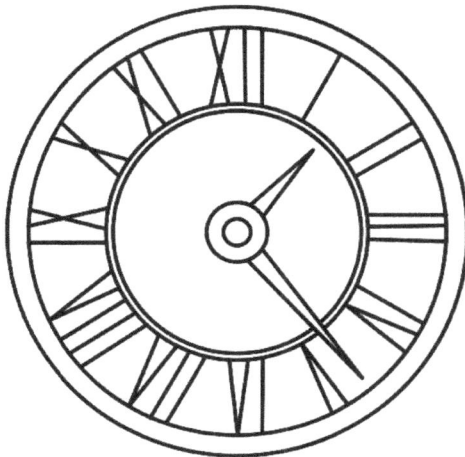

Know Yourself
You know who you are
You know your experiences
You know what you think
Don't ever let other people
Decide that their opinion
On who you are
Is more important than you.

The Turtle and the Tiger Snake

The turtle and the tiger snake
as a pair of friends - unlikely
the turtle was always cautious
while snake was often lawless

Turtle liked to analyse and think
understand the possibilities
while tiger snake just threw itself in
to hell with consequences

Tiger snake found turtles manner
limiting and frustrating
it tried to allow the turtle time
but the now was just not waiting

What tiger snake didn't understand
was why turtle liked to plan
its life before they had met
had been a complete chaotic mess

Turtle had previously been caught up
in the coils of an English adder
who didn't allow turtle to have a voice
or say in anything that mattered.

So turtle learnt to strategise
it created a sense of safety
a tiny amount of control
over a life that has been spinning wildly

But tiger snake did not appreciate
turtles' insistence on analysing
it just wanted to be in the now
missing out was agonising

Eventually tiger snake grew tired
and turtle grew more anxious
the tiger snake kept on insisting
the turtle give up its planning

Turtle felt it was not being heard
snake joked about never hearing
turtle kept on compromising
and tiger snake kept demanding

Neither felt each other heard
turtle felt it had no say
many offensive words were spoken
and they decided to part ways

This split from friendship was very nasty
turtle withdrew into its shell
as the tiger snake had tried to bite it
for having the audacity to rebel

2 years passed, there was no forgiving
turtle could not take a chance
then it heard through the grapevine
that tiger snake has met its match

It turned out snake took too many risks
and did not think of consequence
the tiger snake had met its karma
its ego now drying on the fence.

Bad Man

You want to know what sort of man you are
go find a mirror
look into those whisky coloured eyes
staring back at you.

Looking back at you
is a man
who was offended
by the death of a child
who demanded an apology
from that child's mother
who said he wouldn't send a
'happy death day' message –
whatever the fuck you think that is

Peering out at you
is a man
who demanded that child
is never mentioned again
who told that mother she was selfish
because she 'let' her child
die on your birthday
ruining it for you
seven years before she met you,
eleven years before she told you.

She didn't have her daughter die
in order to upset you
she certainly didn't select
the fourth of June for her death
she wasn't sitting there
rifling through a calendar
selecting the perfect date
thinking, hey I know
I'll have her die on that date
it's the birthday of that friend
that I haven't met yet

For years she never told you,
never made a big deal
other than writing about it
on Facebook every year
How do you think she felt
when you made those demands of her
did you even stop and think
before you let those words escape?
Horrendously selfish
Disgustingly callous
What a choice you gave her –
your birthday or her child's death

Look deep into those eyes of whisky
staring back at you
Ask yourself –
what sort of man
would be offended
by the death of a child.

What kind of man are you?

Silver Linings

I always looked for happiness
even when my life was dark.
I always searched for silver linings
when everything was hard.

You told me finding those seeds of joy
was a sign that I was crazy.
That finding happiness when times were tough
was showing my insanity

Why did you want me to take myself
and throw happiness away?
Why did you say that me trying to be happy
was a fucked-up thing to say?

Why would you want me to choose
the dark over the light?
Why would you want me to fail
and not put up a fight?

Who are you to say that looking
for joy was oh, so wrong?
Who are you to tell me
that my happiness should be gone?

Broken Masks

When the mask starts to slip
and their personality flips
you start to see underneath
why they didn't make any sense

I started to listen
with horror arising
as he started to tell me
all about his new girlfriend
all these things I didn't want
or ever need to know
about the first time they had sex
and her poor oral skills
that he didn't like her son
he found him very weird
didn't want him around
he shouldn't be in society
I stopped and I stepped back
the horror, it was growing

He insinuated his girlfriend
had been a promiscuous slut
never dated anyone for years
from the time of her divorce
just slept with random strangers
from tinder every month

Who the hell talks about
A new partner like that?!

He sat there and told me with glee
about how he had quite purposely
been nasty and horrid
and rude to her face
nice one day, nasty the next
he was testing how much
she'd actually put up with,
and see how much
she actually liked him

If she did not appreciate
his nasty demeanour
he'd walk way briskly
as she'd not be for him
who cared if he hurt her
or made her confused
he needed to know
she'd always be nice to him.

There's only one phrase
that clearly defines
that clearly screams out
what that behaviour is called
making sure she won't leave

if he's being disgusting
that is what's known as
abuse conditioning

Every time he started bragging
about how healthy they were
everything he was saying
went from bad to even worse

He got her to agree
that as a sign of her trust
she'd tell him everyone she'd seen
and interacted with daily
and if he was unhappy
with the people she saw
she'd cease talking to them
for the rest of her days

If her friends didn't like him
if they thought himself odd
she would drop them immediately
no matter how close they were

Then told me in excessive detail
How she had agreed,
if they didn't work out
she'd forever stay single

that he was her last stop
in her life's love train
if she broke up with him
never date anyone again

It got worse and worse
as the days turned to weeks
apparently, she was unable to make
decisions without him

When I finally met her
she seemed fairly nice
then I watched and I heard her
put herself down
that he was so smart
and she was just stupid,
that he was her brains
her intelligence excluded.

Little Bird

The little bird perched
in its gilded cage fine
the door was left open
but it did not want to fly out

Every time it decided
it wanted to be free
it was told that it's own mind
was not what it should be

It was told what to think
it was told what to chirp
it was told that its feelings
were not what they were

Little bird wanted out
but was convinced it was safer
to remain in its cage
mayhap fly away later

This little bird desired
to live and be free
but it wasn't being caged
by the physical things

Its identity was denied
by those who said love
as they had placed chains
on the mind of a dove.

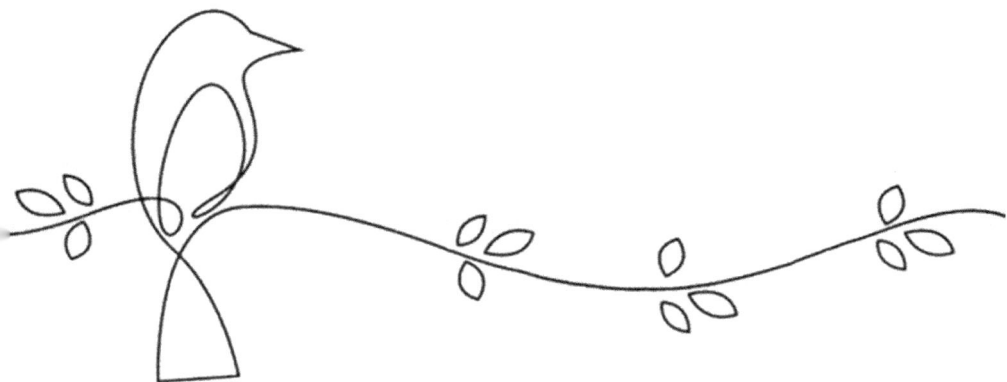

Importance

Are you but a single drop of water,
within the endless universe.
Are you but a thought, inside an idea,
in a flash of light.
Are you but a brief moment
within the vast oceans of time.
Are you but a chirp of sound,
Without echo in the night.
or are you just random interconnectedness
of random atoms almost empty
appearing in the same random space
within the infinite void of nothing.

toxic/empathy

mean
toxic
abusive
ultimations
invalidation intimidation

---

feeling perceiving kind heart believing
understanding
empathy
caring
love

Walk

I should have walked away
the first time you raised your voice
when you flipped from nice to angry
at the bottom of Schlinks Pass

I should have walked away
the first time you raised your fist
but we were in the middle of nowhere
with no one to assist

I should have walked away
when you kept calling me a bitch
and when I asked you not to
it was a joke – and you persisted

I should have walked away
when the first time an issue I raised
your first response was red hot anger
and ultimations on how to behave

I should have walked away
when the first time you made me cry
your response was deathly silence
after you had tried to justify

I should have walked away
when I worked out I meant nothing
that not one of your friends or family
even knew that I existed

I should have walked away
when we were in Newcastle biking
and I woke up with your hand
around my neck and I was choking

I should have walked away
after the weekend in Coffs Harbour
where your nasty demeaning behaviour
meant that leaving felt much safer

The first time I walked away
was when your presence made me anxious
that a message with your name on
resulted in throwing up in the toilet

I should have stayed away
but I wanted to believe
so I told myself you weren't that bad
and you said the issue was me

I should have walked away
when you derided my daughters' death
but I didn't, and I regret it
because it meant you did it again.

I should have walked away
between the first time and the last
all those times my finger hovered over
the button that said block

I should have walked away
and I should have kept on walking
I should have never let you back in
so you could keep destroying

I should have walked away
when you told me my own thoughts
where my feelings and what I wanted
were being assigned to me by you

Eventually I didn't walk
eventually I bolted
as a person that treats other people like that
should always be avoided.

Red Flags

You're the type of person
who makes threats to a woman
if she doesn't do as she told she'll be beaten
You're the type of person
who undermines another being
that's the only way you make yourself feel better
You're the type of person
who devolves to angry violence
when someone chooses to not take your guidance
You're the type of person
who refuses to be held accountable
for the words and actions you took
You're the type of person
who blames everyone around them
instead of looking at your own behaviours
You're the type of person
who will make out that they're a victim
when someone rightly holds you to answer
You're the type of person
who will destroy another human
for having ideas that are different to yours
You're the type of person
whose red flags are waving madly
you only have to step back and look.

You Did Not Know Me

It funny that you thought
you ever really knew me
you didn't know what I am like
when I am actually happy

I like to dance and sing
and make up silly lyrics
cleaning the whole house
with Guns 'n' Roses playing

I like to do the crosswords
solve a few sudoku
read books by Stephen King
or even trashy novels

I've always been an introvert
I don't like being in crowds
I prefer to stick to corners
when I am going out

I should have listened to my friends
and definitely to my family
my family thought you rather odd
and my friends didn't really like you

They didn't like the way I was
when I was in your presence
as I folded into myself
lost my effervescence

They didn't like the way
that you liked to talk over me
that you deliberately sat yourself
between me and everybody

They didn't like the way
I collapsed into myself
I wasn't me around you
I was far less than myself.

Dance Of Death

The toxic and the empathetic
locked in a dance of death
the empathetic good and true
believing everything toxic says
the toxic individual
100% sure they're always right
that everyone around them
is also telling lies.

The toxic person waltzing
their dance of death eternal
leaving a trail of wreckened corpses
alongside their path of life infernal
each one twirled intricately
aware that empathy is blind
as he choreographed their lives
through the manipulation of their minds.

Care Less

Maybe you should have known
maybe you should have realised
the things that you were doing
would lead to our demise

Maybe you should have thought
maybe you should have listened
I kept on trying to tell you
but you refused to hear

Maybe you should have seen
maybe you should have accepted
that your wordless contradictions
would result in trust to end

Maybe you should have deduced
maybe you should have reasoned
that your continuing self-obsession
would cause your own downfall

Maybe you should have noticed
maybe you should have considered
that the people you keep hurting
would eventually just leave

Maybe you should have known
maybe you should have awareness
but to be able to understand it
you'd actually have to care.

Unsuspecting

Maybe I was naïve
maybe I was trusting
as when you said you cared
I didn't realise you were lying

Maybe I was sincere
maybe I was sheltered
as you justified your threats
I accepted the fault was mine

Maybe I was honest
maybe I was unwary
as I gave you all my trust
and you became an adversary

Maybe I was blind
maybe I just believed
as I thought that you were good
but you proved I was mistaken

maybe I was unsuspicious
maybe I was true
as my ability to love
turned out to be wasted on you.

Castle

She lived in a castle, so beautiful and vast
where there were no fences to keep others out
she welcomed strangers to come visit and stay
making new friends, some remaining for days

Along came some people that turned out to be bad
who attempted to rob her and make her feel sad
she started to build fences, keep some of them out
a small fence to start with, made of clear glass

One of these strangers, he showed special interest
he was so nice, he was just different
he was her prince, in love she did fall
convinced her their love required a new wall

At the edge of her realm, a wall he built high
it kept others out but also kept her inside
strangers turned away, her friends were removed
her prince was controlling and he disapproved

Eventually she saw her life was a mess
her prince had dug tunnels under her parapets
her foundations unstable, her walls were atilt
she banished the prince, and started to rebuild

She built herself new walls, up close to her castle
made out of stone, with doors and with windows
she could see out, and others see in
still thought that strangers could be trusted friends

A new stranger stood at her walls and demanded
that he should be let in, he wasn't a danger
how dare that she think that, her walls were unfair
he wasn't the prince, how could she compare

She opened a door, let this stranger inside
straight through her walls, she had nothing to hide
walls that he demanded had to be ripped down
as he should have access to her entire compound

This stranger was friendly, but criticised smugly
advised she remodel, her castle was ugly
too late she realised this stranger was evil
a nice-looking man who was hiding a demon

She built some new walls, solid and slick
twenty feet tall and a hundred feet thick
a wide deep moat dug, filled with carnivorous fish
a fire breathing dragon, and a cavernous abyss

She sits alone now, in her castle so high
not trusting strangers, only friends wander by
she'd sometimes feel lonely, but rather feel safe
her castle, her sanctuary, an impenetrable place.

Forgive Me

You'll never be able to look me in the eyes
and tell me that you're sorry
You'll never be able to admit the things you did
were really, truly disturbing
You'll never be able to look at others
and care that you caused them pain
You'll never be able to admit
your words and actions were to blame

I will never hear you apologise
I will never hear your truth
I will never hear your explanation
about why you do the things you do

You made a massive impact on my life
I remember some days with fondness
but while some of it was pleasant
so much of it - horrendous

So, as I close the book on you
and put it away up on my shelf
I forgive myself for loving you
as love was not at fault

I loved you as my mother
I loved you as my spouse

I loved you as my friend
but love was not enough

As love is never anger
and love is never hurt
love is never controlling
by threatening to leave or worse

I forgive myself for caring
I forgive myself for snapping
I forgive myself for the knots I tied
as I tried to keep you happy

I forgive myself for believing
I forgive myself for trying
I forgive myself for being blind
to all the times that you were lying

I forgive myself for ignoring flags
I forgive myself for disregarding
all the times that you showed me truth
by the actions you were taking

I loved you truly, I loved you well
and I am not ashamed
as I treated you with honesty
while you were toxic unrestrained.

Resilience

On a rocky stony cliff
overlooking the ocean blue
a little yellow gerbera grows
in a crack of dirt within the stone.

Buffeted by salty winds
soaked by ocean waves
the little yellow gerbera holds on
quietly growing all alone.

It doesn't matter how strong the winds become
or how high the waves are storming
that little yellow gerbera keeps growing
its face towards the sun.

Ten Million

You had ten million chances
and ten million more
to do the right thing by me.
I may be empathetic, loving and caring
but underneath all of that is hidden
a solid unyielding spine
of weapons grade titanium
it's unbending, unforgiving and strong.
If that spine is uncovered
there will be no more forgiving
for the hurt and bullshit you do.
As you had ten million chances
and ten million more
and you used every one of them.

Your lies and gaslighting
unreliability and violence
made me feel unwanted and worthless.
All of them taking
one of your many chances
my empathy and forgiveness unending.
The more that you threatened
and threw ultimations
the less of my empathy was left.
You seemed so surprised
when I walked out of your life

never again to return.
But you had ten million chances
and ten million more
now there's not a single one left.

The Phoenix

Too many times you broke me apart
Too many times you destroyed my faith
Too many times you burnt me down
But as you sifted through the ashes
of what was left behind
trampling what little remained
you failed to find me.

You failed to see what lay beneath
You failed to see the truth of me
Hidden within the destruction I lay waiting,
barely breathing
as you walked away
confident in the devastation you left
I waited.

Hardly moving,
my inner self dark and dim,
I waited.
As the ashes shifted,
revealing what was left,
I waited.

Waited until safety was clear
Waited until you were gone

Then slowly, carefully I looked about,
allowing myself to start shining
hesitant,
and yet stronger, smarter.

Unfurling my wings,
starting to burn brighter every day
because I am the phoenix,
beautiful and fierce
You did not see my inner strength
You did not see my inner soul
You did not break me in the end
because I am stronger than even you believed.

I am the phoenix.

And I am free.

Toxic Behaviours

· A dictionary of toxic behaviours ·

This section is a dictionary list of the toxic behaviours described in the poetry. This list is not exhaustive to all toxic types of behaviour, as there are many more types of toxicity. This dictionary should be used in addition to other reading to gain a thorough understanding of what toxic people do.

Belittling

The act of making someone feel small, and that their accomplishments, thoughts, feelings, or experiences are unimportant or unworthy of being mentioned. Belittling comments are often passive-aggressive or cruel.

Examples:

I know you're good at your job, but you're just a Business Analyst, not as respected as a developer.

You're just a girl, obviously maths is too hard for you to understand.

Congratulations on the job, but know you only got that job because of me.

You wouldn't know what real work is, your job involves sitting on your arse, not real manual work.

Blame Shifting

A key characteristic of toxic people is an inability to accept responsibility or accountability for their own actions or words. They shift the blame onto other people as they are too ashamed to face that they may have been in the wrong. It is a defence mechanism to ensure that their own shaky low self-esteem is maintained.

Toxic people will often accuse a person that is trying to resolve an issue, of blaming shifting onto them – another way to put the person on the back foot to defend themselves, preventing resolving the issue, as the toxic person has now tried to avoid accountability by blaming the other person for doing what they are doing themselves.

Examples:

I had to be unreliable, look at what you were doing, if only you weren't so frustrating, I wouldn't have to do that.

I didn't do anything wrong, look at yourself, your mental health issues are making you confuse me with your ex-husband and you're being unfair. Why are you doing this to me?"

Coercive Control

A pattern of using a variety of behaviours to control someone's behaviours, through exerting power and causing fear. The behaviours are within the other forms of toxic behaviours, but also come with the threat of bad outcomes for the person if they fail to meet the toxic persons expectations. Threats to leave them, threats to hurt them, threats that the person or their loved ones or belongings will be damaged. This is straight out emotional abuse and is considered a crime in most states of Australia.

Examples:

You kids better talk to me nicely, or I'll cut all the head off your toys and throw them away.

If you talk about your whisky, I'll get upset, and if I get upset my girlfriend has done six years of boxing and she's very protective of me.

If you tell me I'm wrong, there will be consequences you won't like.

If you roll your eyes, or touch your hair in a way I don't like, I'll get angry, and you don't want to see me angry.

Constant Criticism

A steady, ongoing negativity about their personality, their performance, behaviours – focussing on all the things that they are doing wrong, or need to improve. Continual and constant criticism destroys self-esteem, undermines motivation, and causes significant impacts on mental health.

Examples:

You're not maternal at all. If I left the children with you, your complete lack of being a mother will ensure they are dead in a week.

Oh, I see you haven't finished cleaning before I turned up. Time got away from you?

Constant Need for Validation

A common sign for toxic self-absorbed individuals is their constant need to be admired or validated by others. They often exaggerate their achievements, or ongoing bragging about things that turn out to be fiction in an effort to gain praise and boost their ego. In truly toxic individuals, this constant need covers their false self – the persona they created to prove they are worthy to themselves.

Examples:

I went skydiving once, did two jumps. The instructors said I was the best student they ever had, they were amazed at my skill, I could have done it solo immediately.

The people at that speaker company stole my idea for that subwoofer. They knew I was right and instead of giving me kudos, they stole it (but had zero contact with said company ever).

Controlling

A controlling person is someone who attempts to create and maintain control, authority, and/or decision-making power over other people to get them to conform to their own needs and desires through different forms of manipulation. Controlling behaviour can include everything from directly telling someone what they can or cannot do to more discreet methods like guilt-tripping, gaslighting, passive-aggressive comments, possessiveness, constant criticism, or jealousy.

A controlling person will undermine your confidence and make you feel insecure, putting you down in private and/or public. They might criticise the way you dress or how you spend your time, exaggerate your 'flaws', or make fun of you in front of others but pass it off as 'just a joke.' Extreme methods of control include ultimations, silent treatments or stonewalling, and threats.

Crazy Making

The ultimate in the toxic behaviour suite – making some feel like they are going crazy. This includes many of the other toxic behaviours – gaslighting, manipulation, lying, controlling and invalidation. A crazy-makers will put you in a lose-lose situation and then blame you for it. They are inconsistent, unreliable, and usually will have a very selective memory (at least when interacting with you). They will get you in a situation where they give you two options, and when you choose one they berate you for not choosing the right one – but if you'd chosen the other the outcome would have still been the same. You can do nothing right – you are given the illusion of choice, and the toxic person will deny even giving you a choice. There is no way to win in this situation.

Define Who You Are

Complete devaluation – where the toxic person is defining who you are, what you think, what you feel, what you want. Your actual feelings and beliefs are told to be wrong. That you don't know yourself, and they know you better than you know you.

Part of this can be being accused that you are still in love with someone when you aren't, or doing things or buying things due to your 'ongoing obsession with them' or a need to 'show them you still want them'. You have to accept their version of who you are, or they will get angry at you. You no longer exist in your own mind.

It's a reflection of their own self-obsession, ego and desire to be in complete control. They can't comprehend that you have your own likes, thoughts outside of them, and buy things or do

187

things for you – if they can define who you are, and what you think, then they are in complete control of you, and you won't leave them or argue with them.

Devaluation

Toxic people are known to devalue others through dismissive remarks or hostile humour, or treat them as beneath them to make them feel subhuman and alone. They may also classify others as inferior, not as smart, unworthy, or crazy to justify attacking them, or to influence others to attack them or not have anything to do with them.

Toxic people will talk badly about anyone and everyone, brag about hurting those people, and even use that devaluation to manipulate others. Be aware, if they talk negatively about others, they will talk negatively about you as well.

Financial Abuse

Money is the root of all evil, so they say. Toxic people can use money, and your access to it to exploit you, or to abuse you. In a relationship, the access to money can be used to manipulate you, or keep you in a situation where you can't leave as they have removed your ability to access funds at all.

Financial exploitation and abuse include such things as: controlling or spending your money, ruining your credit history, feeling entitled to your money, criticising or controlling your job and where you work, sabotaging your work, preventing you from going to work, criticising your financial abilities, loaning money from you and playing games in paying you back, demanding you require their permission to spend money while spending it themselves, and even hiding your funds from you.

Gaslighting

Gaslighting is one of most insidious forms of toxic and abusive behaviours. The victim is driven to the point that they start questioning their own memory resulting in low self-esteem, reduced confidence in their own abilities, learned helplessness, and a pervasive need and reliance on the toxic person to validate reality.

The toxic person continuously denies what happened, inserting their own versions, which normally makes them unaccountable for the things that are not right. Their absolute confidence that they are right and the victim is wrong - even when the victim has unassailable evidence- coupled with the victim wanting the toxic person to be happy and avoid arguing, results in the victim apologising for the error and internalising blame. Victims feel helpless, worthless, and powerless and question their own sanity.

Grandiose Ego

An exaggerated sense of self, and belief in their own superiority, knowledge, importance, or identity, often coupled with the belief that other people are jealous of them. People that show a grandiose ego believe themselves to be better than other people and look down upon others as inferior. This leads to them taking risks and doing things believing they won't get caught due to their smarter than average intellect.

toxic/empathy

Hot and Cold Behaviours

Where a person will be overly attentive and affectionate, and then flip into being cold, distant, and unresponsive. Nice one day, nasty the next.

This is straight out manipulation, as they want to see how hard you will try to win them back, they want you to chase and ignore that they have treated you badly.

It creates feelings of insecurity, and can also result in a *trauma bond*, and ensures you stay in a toxic situation for far longer than you should have. Our need and wish to be loved and respected leads us to ignore their cold indifference and we focus on the small signs that they might care about us instead. When treated nicely, you dare to hope, only to have them flip and crush us when they start to withholding their attention again. It is a seemingly endless rollercoaster ride with no opportunity to get off.

Insincerity

Saying things that you don't actually mean or feel. This is deception and hypocrisy. An insincere person is not genuine, and is often phony or dishonest. Insincerity comes across as falseness or hollowness.

Invalidation

Emotional invalidation is the act of dismissing or rejecting someone's thoughts, feelings, or behaviours. Invalidation is used to slowly erase you. After all, when you've been emptied of your identity, full compliance to the toxic persons demands is almost guaranteed. You will do anything at all to stay in the toxic persons good books.

Invalidation includes: Denial, flipping the focus onto you, dismissiveness of your feelings, being judged as deficient in some way, and worst – being told that your beliefs about your own feelings are wrong and that the toxic person knows what you think, feel, or want better than you do. They have erased you completely and you now are what they say you are. If you fight back, they will call you crazy. Their version of you is the only allowable reality.

Lack of Accountability

Classic toxic behaviour where the person refuses to take any responsibility for their own actions or words. This refusal to acknowledge their own shortcomings results in the toxic person deflecting or shifting blame onto others. It is never they fault, they didn't do anything, if only the other person had done something first, if only their employer understood them better. Excuses after excuses about why they cannot be held accountable for anything at all.

Lack of Empathy

The hallmark of narcissism is the lack of empathy to other people, the inability to understand, or even care, how someone is feeling, or how your actions affect them. They can learn to mimic empathy, they know what it looks like and how it sounds, but it always comes off a little off and jilted. The lack of empathy will really be hard to miss in times of stress or when the event is not about them.

People with low or no empathy are quick to criticise, refuse to apologise, avoid emotional situations, have difficulty in sharing in someone else's success, and are quite averse to understanding someone else's grief. They just do not particularly care what others think or feel.

Manipulation

Manipulation will come in many forms, and is one of the harder toxic behaviours to detect as most of the times it is insidious and comes across as well-meaning advice or slight passive aggressiveness. Where there a multiple people involved, the manipulator will play them off each other – in intimate relationships this can be triangulation – using the traits of the other to demean someone, or use them to put another down, or even to deride them so the third person does not want to talk to them anymore. Manipulation is emotional and mental abuse, that uses one's person good intentions to coerce them into doing what the manipulator wants. In very toxic manipulators, they will drive the other person into only being able to trust what the manipulator says, at the expense of all other relationships, destroying the person sense of self and self- esteem.

Masking / Mirroring

Mirroring is where a person starts to copy and mimic the other persons behaviours and mannerisms. A toxic person does this, as they know the other person will feel a greater rapport with them, and bring down their walls and boundaries quicker. It is a manipulation technique to gain someone sense of trust and a sense of intimacy where one would not have existed. Many people that have experienced this effect talk about how safe they felt at the beginning, how their walls just weren't needed because it was like they were the completed part of themselves.

Which leads to masking – the mask that the toxic person wears to hide their true personality. Their true sense is likely to be vulnerable and insecure – or just completely lacking, a void. The toxic person wears masks of other people they admire or like as it gives them a sense of belonging where their true self wouldn't get the same. A mirror is a type of mask.

Neglect

Toxic people that are so wrapped up in themselves, they are unable to even consider the needs of someone else, let alone ensure that the other persons needs are being met. Most obvious in parental or intimate relationships, neglect can be physical, emotional, or mental. The silent treatment is a form of emotional neglect, where as restricting access to food, shelter and safety are all forms of physical neglect. Toxic people will put their needs as the defining nexus of the relationship, at the expense of everyone else.

Nothing is ever Good Enough

You do your best. You win an award. You get published in a newspaper. Your boss praises your work. You get a raise, a promotion. But the toxic person in your life tells you, and shows you that your achievements are less than, they aren't good enough to get their praise. They dismiss it as unimportant, mock it, downplay it, or even claim that you were unable to achieve it without them. Some toxic people even attempt to claim your accomplishments as their own.

Everything you do is never good enough: your school grades aren't good enough, your humour isn't funny enough, you aren't attractive enough, thin enough, not enough like them. You spend years trying to change yourself, just be enough.

Parentification

Parentification is the role reversal where the person who is the parent expects the child to look after them. The child becomes the emotional and/or physical care giver of their parent, which disrupts the child's own self development, maturing, connections with their peer group and creates a psyche built on putting others needs before their own. It is emotional neglect and abuse.

Parentification can lead to life-long traumas, anxieties, and an inability to form lasting relationships due to not developing the appropriate skills to create and maintain boundaries, poor self-esteem, hyper self- reliance, and overreliance on others validation that they are 'doing the right thing'

Pathological Lying

Continuously lying without a clear motive. Pathological lying is a compulsion to lie about even innocuous things, with no apparent purpose. The liar presents themselves in the lies in a consistent favourable light either as the hero or as the undeserving victim.

The lies cover anything at all: from the last conversation you may have had, to their job, their past, or an argument with their significant other. Coupled with gaslighting, a pathological liar will do a lot of damage to their unknowing victims.

Physical Abuse

When a person exerting control over another person through the use, or threat, of physical force. Physical abuse covers a large range of behaviours including punching, kicking, hitting, pinching or other activities intended to causes physical pain, but also to limit the other persons self-determination.

Physical abuse also covers acts such as using physical actions near the other person such as throwing things, punching the wall, smashing things intending to make the victim scared.

Threats of physical violence will have the same intended effect as actual physical acts, in terms of controlling the victim by making them afraid.

Playing the Victim

This behaviour encompasses several of the other toxic traits: namely entitlement, constant needs for validation, blame shifting, grandiose ego and projection. This behaviour is very recognisable where something has not gone the toxic persons way and they create sob stories about why they didn't get what they expected/thought they were entitled to. A missed job promotion will be written off as the manager being jealous and protecting their own job, a termination of a job made out to be due to a toxic workplace culture, a request to fill in a timesheet the same as everyone else made out to be the manager lacking trust in them. They are victims to feeling attacked by the consequences of their own actions – so they are not to blame.

Projection

This is defence mechanism to protect their own inner self, used to deflect and project their own behaviours and traits onto the other person. The toxic person is chronically unable to see their behaviours as wrong and will use anything to avoid being held accountable for them. Projecting cheating, abusive behaviours as a trait of the victim and they are the poor abused partner.

Examples:

Accusing their partner of cheating, when they are doing it themselves

Angrily telling someone they are a liar, when the toxic person was lying and got caught out.

Informing new partners how horrible an ex-partner was, describing all the things they personally did as traits of the ex.

Reactive Abuse

A manipulation tactic used by perpetrators of abuse to convince both the victim of abuse and others that they are the ones being abused. It occurs when the person being abused reacts strongly to the abuse they are suffering, perhaps choosing to argue back or physically defend themselves from the person abusing them. Once they do this, the person abusing them uses it as an example or "proof" that they are being abused, and that the person being abused is to blame. They can also use it as evidence that you are mentally ill, or crazy.

They can then use this scenario later as a threat to win arguments, keep the person they're abusing at bay, or as a bid to maintain their power. If it happens enough, the gaslighting can be so harmful that it starts to convince the person being abused that they really are to blame and that they are a bad person.

Sabotaging Events

Toxic people have difficulty in other people enjoying themselves, and go out of their way to undermine other people's achievements, events, birthdays, even funerals.
They may take an upcoming event that they know you are looking forward to and provoke an argument to get you to cancel. Or insinuate that you yourself will do things to ruin the event and that you need to watch what your doing – anything to make the event worse for you.

They will make themselves the focus of your birthday, bringing negativity into what should be a happy event, or make funerals about themselves by introducing new partners not even 5 minutes before the start and using the event to brag about their relationship.

Silent Treatment / Stonewalling

A classic sign of a toxic individual, who uses silence to manipulate others, and punish them. If they perceive you've done the wrong thing to them, instead of talking about it to you, they'll punish you be refusing to engage with you at all. This is considered an extreme form of emotional abuse. It's highly disrespectful and leads to a loss of self-esteem and heightened anxiety. Often the toxic person uses this to force behaviour changes – told their done the wrong thing, the toxic person gets angry and then refuses to talk for days or even weeks, the other person learns not to bring up issues. The toxic person both avoids having their own poor behaviours addressed and will also have the power in the relationship.

Smear Campaigns

Smear campaigns are used to isolate you and control how others view you and sympathise with the toxic person. It's psychological warfare, often started months or even years before the other person becomes aware and tries to walk away from them. This can happen with family, friends, work colleagues and intimate partners.

The ultimate objective of the smear campaigns is to establish domination over their target by spreading rumours, false allegations, and malevolent gossip to manipulate others into disbelieving the victim. The victim of the campaign is left defending themselves, losing their support network and being isolated. A victim speaking the truth is not a smear campaign – smears are based on falsity – victims have evidence to support reality. Victims will try to explain situations and their feelings, toxic people will blame the other.

Sprinkle the Truth

Scattering truths within their exaggerated stories of themselves. This is used effectively as they will point at the truth to make out the rest is also true – used very well in propaganda, and

Example:
"I'm a contract HTML developer, I earn really good money, more than you" where the truth is they are a developer and the rest is false.

Surveillance/Stalking

Both online and physically, a toxic person monitors where you are, or what you're doing. They use this to get information on you, to either know where you might be, or to use against you later. Toxic people are more likely to be social media 'quiet' – having accounts across all the major platforms, but rarely posting themselves. This gives them anonymity, the ability to search and view at will, and doesn't allow others to find out things about them.

Stalking is the next level, where the toxic person will physically turn up where you are, contact your friends or family wanting information on you, or befriend them in an effort to get to you. The IT savvy toxic individual may attempt to hack into your computer network to digitally spy on your activities without your knowledge.

Taking Credit

Toxic people love to get praise, and what better way than overstating their own efforts, claim credit for other people's work, or insinuate only their efforts made the outcome possible. Inversely, they are quick to blame others when something fails, lacking accountability for their own actions when things do not work out. If you attempt to correct the record, and show that your work was taken, the toxic person will argue and dismiss all the evidence you have proving your claim, and may call you crazy for even doubting them.

Trauma Bonding

Trauma bonding is a psychological response to abuse/toxic behaviours. It a occurs when a person forms a connection or relationship with the person who abuses them through a develops out of a repeated cycle of abuse, devaluation, and positive reinforcement.

A trauma bond creates an addiction – considered worse than heroin to overcome, as the cycle of nice and nasty releases dopamine into the system each time they are nice to you. You might find that you blame yourself for what's happening, especially if reinforced by the toxic person. That can allow you to keep seeing the toxic person as good and you see yourself as inadequate.

If a toxic person starts the relationship with a nice/nasty cycle, it's not love, it's addiction.

Twisting Words

Used as both manipulation and gaslighting, the toxic person intentionally repeats your words back at you but in a different manner to make the intent of your words have a different meaning. This also includes elements of victim-blaming and fact distortion, and can include them redefining words to suit themselves instead of accepted English dictionary definitions.

Walking on Eggshells

When you start thinking about how to phrase a question or statement to someone, because you know a single word or phrase, or even your tone of voice or body language will set of a barrage of negativity towards you. You're careful how you approach them, careful what you say because their explosive, erratic, and sometimes even violent behaviour in response is frightening.

Signs of this include:

Heightened anxiety when you need to discuss something with them.

You start preferring to stay silent, instead of addressing an issue, as it's not worth the stress.

Their immediate response to any issues you raise is anger or blame.

You feel unhappy, insecure, powerless or weak

You are always trying to understand their points, make excuses for their behaviour and feel your opinions aren't appreciated or heard

Words and Actions Don't Match

Confusion. Contradiction. Inconsistency. Unreliability.

The toxic person says one thing and does another. You're confused, and bring it up with them. They deny even saying what you know they said – even show them text messages or emails saying exactly that – they deny it – gaslighting. They say they don't like having the radio or music on in the car when driving as its too distractive – then get fined for having too loud music while driving. They make fun of people that buy tiny houses, making derogatory statements – then starts looking at buying one themselves. They say they love you, then do things that they know you don't like. They might be religious or big on charity work, yet drink and do drugs and cheat. Talk about how their children are the most important thing to them, and then refuse to do anything with them.

Being unreliable is manipulation, and lying.

Healing Behaviours

Acceptance

This is a difficult thing to come to terms with – the acceptance that the person you cared about, someone you loved and trusted – exploited and hurt you, and a lot of that was on purpose. Where you have been conditioned to internalise the blame, or had most of the blame of the issue thrust on you, it can be hard to step back from this as realise that you aren't the one that was manipulating another people. You weren't the one hurting someone to absolve yourself of the consequences of their own actions.

Once you can remove the own self-blame of everything that happened, you can start to look at the actual situations, with out the emotions involved, and come to the acceptance that the person you thought they were, and the person they actually are – are two very different things. In a lot of cases with toxic people, the person you thought they were, the person they told you they were – never existed. They were a construct of lies and manipulation, playing on your emotions and exploiting your insecurities.

Know Yourself

Know who you are. If you have spent significant time with a toxic person, it is likely you've spent months or years being told who you are, what your thoughts are, how to think, what to think, even where to work, what you job should be or what you are allowed to wear, or who you can talk to. You have lost yourself.

Be gentle on yourself, finding and knowing yourself can be a long painful process where you must both recognise what is you and what was defined as you. You have been emotionally and psychologically tortured and may even experience PTSD. You lose the ability to trust others, and trust yourself, your memory has been completely questioned and you no longer know what to believe.

Awareness is key. Question your thoughts – are they yours, or what the toxic person said to you? Remove the negative, replace with your own positive ones. You are strong enough to survive, and you can beat the toxic person by defining yourself the way YOU want to be, not the way THEY thought you should be.

Set Boundaries

Its very important to set boundaries over what you will accept and what you won't. Boundaries are about you, and managing your own behaviour; they are setting limits around what an interaction or friendship looks like for yourself.

They are not about telling the other person what to do or say. If you think you are setting a boundary by telling another person "you can't do…." you're being controlling, not setting boundaries. A boundary does not place any responsibility on another person to do, act, or in any way make them behave in way you want them to.

Example:

Boundary: "I do not like to be called names when we are talking, I will end a conversation if there is name calling."

Controlling: "If you talk to me this way, I'm going to get angry and I won't be held accountable for what I do."

Controlling: "You will only talk about these subjects, or I will leave you."

Boundary: "I do not being woken up before 8am, so I will have my phone on silent until then."

Controlling: "I'm telling you not to call me before 8am."

Controlling: "If you call me before 8am, I will tell our friends that you're a psychotic controlling bitch."

Healthy Boundaries are ones that you set for yourself:

I will not accept being friends with someone who constantly lies to me.

I will not be around people who assume my stated boundaries are fake, and so ignore them

I will not date someone who is an alcoholic

Recognise the Signs / Red Flags

This is important – learn how to recognise toxic behaviours from the outset. Many people end up with more toxic people in their lives because they do not know the signs to look for. Most toxic people are wonderfully charming and charismatic people to start off with, and the toxicity ramps up over time until you can no longer recognise the person they are, or the person you have become. The red flags at the beginning are:

Running Hot and cold. Nice, then nasty, then nice

Inconsistency: say or do things that conflict

Expressed desire that their past is off limits

Makes derogatory statements about exes

They get angry when you disagree with them

They talk about their 'bad side' as if its not them

Talk big about the future, tell you you're the one, they never felt this way before, make out you're really special and its been less than 4 months

No Contact

Cut all contact if possible. Starve the toxic person of your presence and start the healing process. You cannot heal well if they are still a part of your life in any manner, as it is far too easy to be pulled back into their toxic world. This can be difficult at the start, but as time goes on and the toxic ties that were created are eroded, you begin to see the behaviours and how bad they were for your own self.

Toxic People Checklist

How they behave

Egotistical

Selfish and self-centred

Entitled

Very few personal possession (i.e. no assets)

Talks about being you "soul mate' early on

Tells you how much you have in common

Tells you they've 'never felt this way before' early

Rushes intimacy

Blows Hot and Cold

Charismatic/charming

Chronic lying

Reckless or impulsive

Drug user and/or alcohol issues

Poor financial management

Talk badly of previous partners

Flashes cash/buys expensive things

Critical of others behind their backs

Tells you personal details of others

Likes to point out your flaws, then help you address them

Inconsistent details of their past

Refusal to talk about their past

Breaks promises

Use the silent treatment/stonewalling

No regards for laws or rules

Difficulty apologising

Anger when confronted

Puts you down in 'jokes'

toxic/empathy

Isolating – expect you to drop friends that don't like them, or
   tells you friends talk badly about you so you drop them
Controlling
Avoids responsibility
Avoids accountability
Belittle / Tries to take ownership of your accomplishments
Gets angry if perceived that people tease them
Boasts about themselves
They must be right, even when they aren't
Compulsive over having the latest technology
Lack integrity
Will talk badly about their work colleagues /managers
Will believe that team successes are only due to their own
   efforts
Borrow money from you, and then play games when they
   need to pay it back
Brags about over-spending
Cheating
Disloyal and two faced – won't have your back
Demands trust
Their stories change
Get angry when you pick up inconsistencies
Talks about being wealthy in the future
Call exes 'crazy' or 'obsessive'
Accused of doing the thing they did / projection
Tries to convince you everyone does what they do
Accuse you of doing things you didn't do
Slander you
Future fakes
Uses words like 'everyone says/knows' to invalidate you
Fake/meaningless apologies

How you might feel

Unsure how they might respond to you

Feel anxious that they might be in a bad mood

Feel like something is wrong

Feel like you need to watch what you say, or how you say it

Feel unsafe

Feel confused

Fear that criticising them will result in a loss of the connection

Take on the blame for difficulties

Feel like you're being judged constantly

Feel pushed into arguments about meaningless things

Constantly feel you need to prove yourself

Start researching their behaviours

Constantly apologising

Your feelings are invalidated or ignored

Your words get twisted in disagreements

Your words are used against you

You never meet their expectations

Afterward

Thank you for reading my book. You may think from my musings that I carry hatred, and perhaps bitterness, for the three people contained within them. I don't. In a way, I pity them.

In the end, they are people - people that I once loved and cared about greatly. People are flawed, they do things and say things that are wonderful, and do and say things that are cruel and hurtful. I walked from all of them, because their presence in my life was destroying me. In the end, I was the only one looking out for myself.

The most glaring similarity with these three, was to this day, every single one of them do not believe that they did anything wrong, in any way.

They are unable to see their own actions as hurtful, and refuse to take responsibility for them. Toxic people are toxic, they just don't see their own behaviours as wrong.

I am not a perfect person, but perfection is unachievable to start with.

Much love,

JL Herald

Your ability to love
is a reflection on you.

Their need to hurt you
is a reflection on them.

Don't confuse the two.